When
FOOTBALL *Was*
FOOTBALL

LEEDS UNITED

First published in 2011

A catalogue record for this book is available from the British Library

ISBN: 978-0-857331-69-4

Published by Haynes Publishing, Sparkford, Yeovil,
Somerset BA22 7JJ, UK
Tel: 01963 442030 Fax: 01963 440001
Int. tel: +44 1963 442030 Int. fax: +44 1963 440001
E-mail: sales@haynes.co.uk
Website: www.haynes.co.uk

Haynes North America Inc., 861 Lawrence Drive,
Newbury Park, California 91320, USA

Images © Mirrorpix

Creative Director: Kevin Gardner
Designed for Haynes by BrainWave

Printed and bound in the US

When
FOOTBALL *Was*
FOOTBALL

LEEDS UNITED

A Nostalgic Look at a Century of the Club

David Walker

Contents

Foreword by John Lukic

I was a 14-year-old schoolboy from Chesterfield in Derbyshire when I arrived for the first time at Elland Road. I'll never forget the experience of turning up for a trial with mighty Leeds.

That was in 1974. The great Don Revie had left to take the England job a few months earlier, Brian Clough had been and gone in 44 days, and Jimmy Armfield was the manager. I can recall there was still an aura about the place. You sensed you were inside a truly great football club. There was still a deep-rooted belief around the club that Leeds were the team all-comers had to beat if they were to achieve success.

When I joined the ground staff two years later I was tutored by Maurice Lindley, who had been a stalwart of Don's backroom staff. Great players such as Norman Hunter, Eddie Gray, Peter Lorimer, Allan Clarke, Paul Reaney, Gordon McQueen, Joe Jordan, David Harvey and Trevor Cherry were still around the club – a living connection to the true glory years. Being a goalie meant that I spent some time with David Harvey, who was a great help to me. He was a brilliant goalie and a great man to look up to. We all respected Dave.

I made my debut as an 18-year-old. Jimmy Armfield had left the club and Jimmy Adamson was in charge. We drew 0-0 at Brighton in a Division One game and it started a record-breaking run for me. I grabbed a place in the club's record books by making 146 consecutive appearances from that debut day. I think the record still stands and I'm proud of it.

When I left Leeds to join Arsenal in 1983 I felt devastated. I was gutted to be moving on. Leeds United was all that I knew. It was the club of my dreams. We'd been relegated a year earlier and, without question, that remains the lowest point of my playing career.

I'll never forget that Tuesday night of misery at West Bromwich Albion. We needed a win to stay up. We lost 2-0. Leeds had problems with their supporters in those days, particularly in the travelling army of fans who followed us everywhere. It was the days of perimeter fences and I recall late in the game at The Hawthorns being aware of the fences behind me shimmering. I wondered what was happening. Then I realized some of the Leeds fans were rocking on the fences, trying to pull them up so they could invade the pitch. A police inspector walked around the back of my goal and said: "Goalie, when the referee blows his whistle I want you to run from this field as fast as you can."

I was 21 when I moved to Highbury and I had seven years at Arsenal before the call came to return to Elland Road. This time I was the club's first £1 million signing. Actually, the fee that was agreed was £995,000 but the Leeds secretary agreed to round the figures up to make it easier to work out the various levies. I'm not sure that was totally appreciated in the Leeds boardroom.

Elland Road was a totally different place 14 years after my first visit. The shadow of Don's great team had proved too much for a number of players and managers down the years. You could never underestimate the achievements of Leeds in the Sixties and

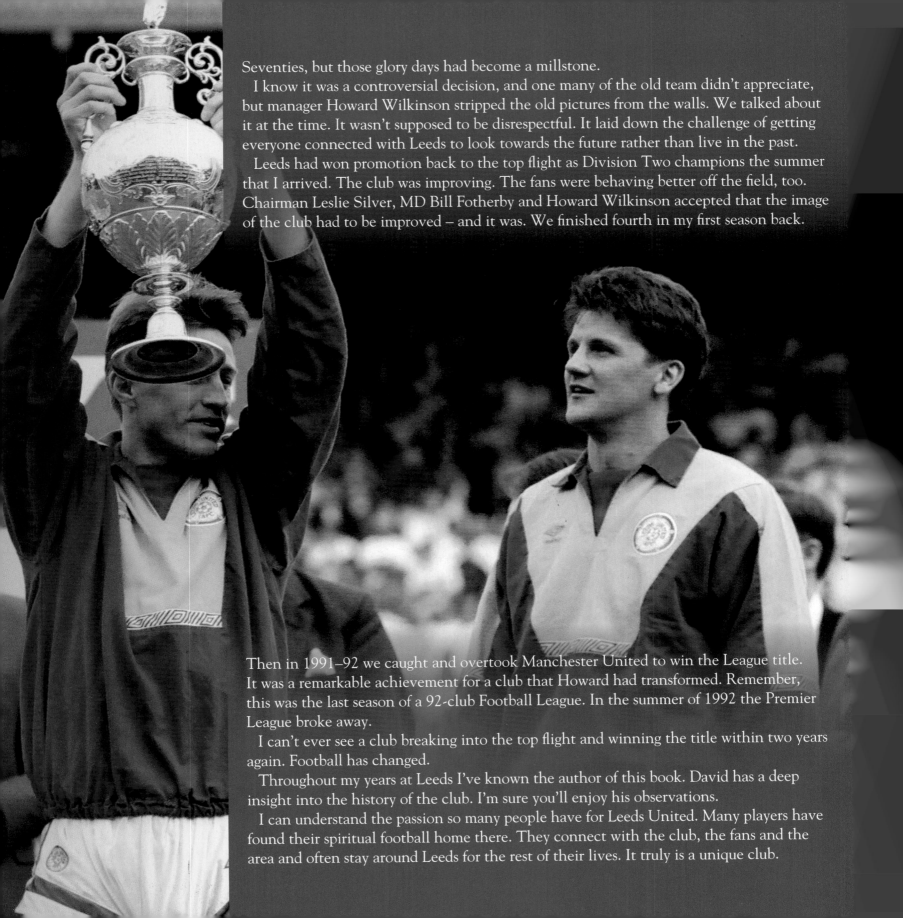

Seventies, but those glory days had become a millstone.

I know it was a controversial decision, and one many of the old team didn't appreciate, but manager Howard Wilkinson stripped the old pictures from the walls. We talked about it at the time. It wasn't supposed to be disrespectful. It laid down the challenge of getting everyone connected with Leeds to look towards the future rather than live in the past.

Leeds had won promotion back to the top flight as Division Two champions the summer that I arrived. The club was improving. The fans were behaving better off the field, too. Chairman Leslie Silver, MD Bill Fotherby and Howard Wilkinson accepted that the image of the club had to be improved – and it was. We finished fourth in my first season back.

Then in 1991–92 we caught and overtook Manchester United to win the League title. It was a remarkable achievement for a club that Howard had transformed. Remember, this was the last season of a 92-club Football League. In the summer of 1992 the Premier League broke away.

I can't ever see a club breaking into the top flight and winning the title within two years again. Football has changed.

Throughout my years at Leeds I've known the author of this book. David has a deep insight into the history of the club. I'm sure you'll enjoy his observations.

I can understand the passion so many people have for Leeds United. Many players have found their spiritual football home there. They connect with the club, the fans and the area and often stay around Leeds for the rest of their lives. It truly is a unique club.

Introduction

Leeds United is a football club that bewitches people. Leeds is the biggest city in Britain that has only one football team, so the focus of every local with a love of the game turns to the progress of the mighty Whites at Elland Road.

That means there are no bragging rights from winning a local derby each season. It's Leeds United against the rest of the world. And Leeds will always be expected to win.

The late, great John Charles summed it up perfectly when reviewing his life as one of the world's greatest players. John said: "I'm a Swansea man born and bred; I enjoyed the most successful time of my career with Juventus in Italy but I played for Leeds and Leeds will always be MY club."

Many old United heroes feel exactly the same way. Leeds United got into their DNA and they were changed for life. In over 30 years as a journalist and five working inside football clubs I've never known any club generate the same level of passion and loyalty from former players as Leeds United. I recall a senior London-based journalist once criticizing Billy Bremner in a bar room debate with Jack Charlton. At the time Jack was the very successful manager of the Republic of Ireland. The days of playing alongside his ginger-haired mate were long gone. Jack had no great reason to fight battles for an old comrade – but, boy, did he put the journalist right in the most uncompromising fashion. Kick Billy, even verbally, and you felt the full force of Jack's size-11 boot sorting you out. The passage of time had not distilled Charlton's loyalty to his great friend and former room-mate.

In a nutshell, that's Leeds United for you. A club where Don Revie instilled the absolute belief that loyalty is paramount. The club that won six major trophies and finished runners-up 11 times between 1964 and 1975. They didn't win all the trophies they deserved. And with the pain of all those last-gasp heroic failures, living with the bitter pangs of disappointment also became part of the club's make-up. Being a Leeds fan, player or manager was never easy. There was pain to be endured along the way. That was always part of the deal.

Elland Road has never been the prettiest or most architecturally striking of grounds but the raw passion generated by a full house has tested the mettle of the most experienced visiting team and inspired even greater levels of commitment from some magnificent Leeds players.

In this book we use the *Daily Mirror* and *Sunday Mirror*'s extensive picture archive. You can visit it online at Mirrorpix. We also use some splendid, old newspaper cuttings from the *Mirror* titles. These can be seen at www.ukpressonline.co.uk.

Leeds United was formed in 1919 following the financial collapse of the original club, Leeds City. Football didn't flourish easily in Leeds. It was, after all, a city renowned for Rugby League.

The arrival of John Charles helped inspire a hint of glory in the Fifties. The fire that burned down the West Stand, and with it the club's administration offices, dressing rooms and medical facilities, exposed the fact that the club was underinsured, and to pay for a new stand John had to be sold to Juventus for a British record fee of £65,000.

Maybe if John had stayed at Leeds the club's next few years would not have been so harrowing, with relegation to the old Division Three looming large at one painful stage. But it was from that low that Revie created a remarkable football empire.

He had been a keen student of the game and had shaped his vision of the future on the way football would develop. Indeed, he was probably the first true players' manager. His rivals tended to be extensions of the boardroom when it came to discussing contracts and players' rights. They were tight and grudging in the days after the abolition of the maximum wage.

Don, who had experienced true poverty during his childhood in Middlesbrough, recognized that looking after the security of his players was a vital part of a manager's make-up. He cared about his players and their families. He got closer to them than any of his rivals. He also wanted them to feel wanted and well rewarded. When he met Johnny Giles to persuade the young Irishman to leave Division One Manchester United to move to Division Two Leeds he offered the player a £60-a-week contract. It was twice the deal he'd been on with the FA Cup holders at Old Trafford. Revie did receive huge financial support from the Leeds

board of the early Sixties. Chairman Harry Reynolds and his directors, dealing with a sizeable overdraft of £250,000, made the recruitment of key men like Giles and Bobby Collins possible. They were inspired signings.

Similarly, 25 years later, when the club was back in the doldrums, chairman Leslie Silver and his fellow board members found the funds to persuade Gordon Strachan to turn down offers from top-flight clubs to provide the on-field inspiration as Leeds stormed out of the old Division Two in 1990 and on to the Division One title in 1992. The city of Leeds historically enjoyed a reputation for canny businessmen. Although directors will never get everything right, the initiative shown by Reynolds and Silver helped make Leeds United one of the most famous clubs in the world.

The Leeds United squad that won the League title for the first time in 1969.

Building A
CLUB

Sharing grounds is nothing new to sports fans in Yorkshire. In Leeds the Headingley Stadium was home to Yorkshire CCC, Leeds RL and more recently the Leeds Carnegie RU team.

Similar ground shares were accepted down the years in Bradford at Park Avenue and Sheffield at Brammall Lane.

The fact is that for many decades the prime winter spectator sport in Leeds was Rugby League. While Leeds were the biggest club there were smaller outfits within the suburbs of Bramley and Hunslet.

Test cricket has been staged at Headingley since 1899. When Don Revie took over at Leeds United in 1961 his club were the second-class citizens in the local sports pecking order. How things were to change.

1904 Leeds City formed. The club play in blue, yellow and white kit. They move into Elland Road following the closure of the Holbeck Rugby Club. 1905 Leeds City elected to the Football League. 1912 Leeds City appoint Herbert Chapman as manager. 1919 Leeds City expelled from the Football League for making illegal payments to players during the First World War. An auction is held at the Metropole Hotel, Leeds. The players and other assets are auctioned off. Billy McLeod raises the most money with his £1,250 move to Notts County. The 16 members of the playing staff moved to nine clubs for £9,250. Leeds United formed on 17th October. They are launched as a non-league club playing in the Midland League. 1920 Leeds United is acquired by Huddersfield Town chairman, Hilton Crowther. He wants to amalgamate the two clubs. A public outcry in Huddersfield wrecks his plan. Huddersfield directors buy Crowther out and he is solely involved in Leeds United. Leeds United are elected to the Football League. They join Division Two. Leeds home kit, given the Huddersfield connection, is blue-and-white stripes. 1923–24 Leeds win the Division Two title and get promotion to the top flight. 1924–25 Leeds struggle and finish in 18th place. 1925–26 This season is even more of a struggle and Leeds just beat relegation. 1926–27 Leeds are relegated. Arthur Fairclough resigns as manager. He is succeeded by his former assistant, Dick Ray. 1927–28 Leeds are promoted back in Ray's first season in charge. They finish as runners-up to Manchester City. 1929–30 A landmark season for Leeds. They finish fifth in the top flight – the club's highest position before Don Revie's reign as manager. 1930–31 The yo-yo team are back. Leeds are relegated from Division One but Wilf Copping makes his United debut. 1931–32 Leeds win promotion back to the top flight. 1934 Copping is transferred to Arsenal. 1934–35 Leeds change kit and start playing in blue-and-yellow halves. 1937–38 Leeds make a

flying start to the season and are among the title contenders but fall away and finish ninth. **1938–39** The last campaign before the Second World War sees Leeds finish 13th. **1946–47** Leeds endure a miserable season. They collect a meagre 18 points and are relegated. Manager Billy Hampson is replaced by former player Willis Edwards. **1947–48** Leeds continue to struggle, with the danger of dropping into Division Three a real possibility. Edwards steps down to assistant manager and is replaced by former Wolves boss, Major Frank Buckley. **1948–49** Leeds finish 15th in Division Two after flirting with relegation. John Charles makes his league debut.

A Dream Comes True

Don Revie's team of the Sixties had consistently created history for Leeds United. But the significance of this picture can not be understated. This was the moment when the Leeds manager and his team celebrated a crowning achievement. They were the champions of England for the first time in the club's history. An incredible achievement given that just a few years earlier, with Revie as a managerial rookie, they had been fighting to escape relegation to the old Third Division.

13

King John

FOOTBALL -STATS-

John Charles

Name: William John Charles CBE

Date of birth: 27th December 1931

Place of birth: Swansea, Wales

Date of death: 24th February 2004 (aged 72)

Position: Centre-half, centre-forward

Leeds career: 1948–57 and 1962

Leeds appearances: 327

Leeds goals: 157

Wales: 38 caps, 15 goals

"
If I picked the best team in the world John Charles would be in it at centre-half and centre-forward. He was that good. I can remember days at Leeds in the Fifties where John was 90 per cent of our side.

Jack Charlton
"

The world's greatest footballer!

By BOB FERRIER

IS he the greatest footballer in the world, this John Charles, centre forward of Leeds United, who has scored twelve goals in seven matches this season?

YOU BET HE IS!

The world is a mighty big parish, and scattered around its corners are some pretty formidable footballers. We have two in this country, quite unlike any others. They are Stanley Matthews and Tom Finney. They are phenomenal, the sorcerers of Soccer, men on a plane apart.

But as a matter of cold opinion, John Charles, the genial giant of Elland-road, is the world's complete footballer.

And he has proved it, for me. As a centre half, his best and preferred position, he was in the Leeds League side at seventeen, in the Wales international side at eighteen.

Goal-Getter

That turbulent Soccer character, Major Buckley, moved him with immediate success to centre forward. He got back into the Wales team—as inside right! Already this season, as centre forward, he has scored two thirds of the Leeds goals!

He is nearly 6ft. 2in., weighs 12st. and a bit. He looks as though he has just been quarried in Carnarvon, or could go fifteen rounds with Marciano without a blush, yet has a smile as quick and fresh as Adlai Stevenson's. He has massive shoulders, slim hips, wears his black shorts hitched very short. For one so huge, he has a very short, quick stride. That gives him exceptional ball control, and he just can't be knocked off the ball. In speed,

JOHN CHARLES
Genial giant of Elland-road.

shooting, heading, he is brilliant, and it is all topped by impeccable style.

But he doesn't know how he does it. "I just go out and play, and enjoy it." He is a completely natural, instinctive footballer.

Raich Carter, his manager, asks: "How could you teach him anything?" and sits mumbling and cursing softly under his breath (Raich does this very well) because he cannot play beside such a man.

Just One Flaw

Ask him about the First Division, and he says, "I suppose every player wants to play there." Club? "Players I talk with say that Arsenal is a great club, but then, Leeds have treated me very well."

That's King Charles.

The only flaw in the canvas is that John is the obsession of team, terrace and town. "Give it to John, and it'll be all right," they say. So far, John has served them very well indeed.

The Reason Why King John Was Sold

The fire at Elland Road in September 1956 was a devastating blow for the club.

The West Stand was gutted. And it was this part of the ground that homed the club offices, dressing rooms and medical facilities. The fact that the club had only limited insurance cover transformed a problem into a full-blown crisis.

The board of directors realized they needed to raise funds to rebuild the main stand. The one major asset that could be sold to do this was star player John Charles. He was acclaimed as one of the best players in the world. Juventus, the establishment club of Italy's Serie A, won the race to sign him.

Leeds could rebuild their ground. They had sold their best player.

Mirror Sport

...ARLES MAY GO
FOR £100,000

...an clubs will ...auction today

By GEORGE HARLEY

...RLES, 25, to another club in this
country," said Mr. Bolton.
"They could pay him no
more than we can. But we
cannot possibly stand in
his way if clubs abroad are
ready to pay him £10,000
or more."

Charles is ready, willing
but not yet able—to go.
His wife, Peggy, will go
into hospital any day now
for the birth of their third
child.

'Golden'

"We expected the baby
today," Charles said last
night. "I would not want
to go to Italy without my
family, and I should have
to wait until the baby is a
few weeks old at least.

"But I don't see how I
could turn down such big
offers from abroad. It
would be a golden oppor-
tunity for me and my
family. We could set our-
selves up for life."

Juventus are ready to
give Charles a two-year
contract and provide a
luxurious flat for him.

Charles, a great centre
half who became a greater
centre forward, would still
be able to play for Wales.

He signed for Leeds in
1949 when he was seven-
teen and gained the first
of his twenty Welsh caps
the following year.

*John Charles signs
for young autograph
hunters outside the
Leeds ground yester-
day. Soon he may be
signing on the dotted
line for Juventus.*

Charles doesn't want to leave Britain, but—

'IT'S TOO TEMPTING
TO TURN
DOWN . .'

By Frank McGhee

BLUNT Sam Bolton,
chairman of Leeds
United, has told the two
Italian clubs competing
for the signature of
centre forward John
Charles:

"You can START the
bidding at £70,000."

This afternoon, he will
be meeting representatives
of the clubs, Internazionale
of Milan, and Juventus of
Turin. The Milan officials
will be travelling up from
Birmingham after their
match in the Midlands last
night

The Juventus boss, hand-
some president Umberto
Agnelli, 22, told me on his
arrival in London last
night that he was worried
and annoyed about his
rivals.

"They are the richest
club in Italy," he said.
"They can pay more
money than we can."

And I think it is unfair
that they should be after
Charles too. We were first.
It was our idea."

He refused to name his
price. "But it is not so
high as the £100,000 sug-
gested in London. Even
John Charles has his
limit."

Charles can expect a flat,
a car and up to £80 a week
in addition to a signing-on
fee of between £10,000 and
£70,000.

'Go to See'

He said on a B.B.C. TV
programme last night that
he did not want to leave
Britain, but the reported
offer was too tempting to
turn down.

"Naturally I will visit
Italy first to see the living
accommodation, if the deal
goes through. But I will
definitely play for Leeds
this Easter," said Charles.

Signor Agnelli assured
me that his club do not
intend to enter into an
auction. "I have fixed a
top price," he said.

Speaking from Birm-
ingham, Dr. Alberto
Valentini, of the Milan
club, says they are will-
ing for Juventus to make
all the running.

"We are interested only
if they fall out of the bidding," he said.

"If they do not buy
him, we may make an
offer. We have informed
Leeds that we are inter-
ested."

17

La Dolce Vita

John Charles wondered what he was walking into when he joined Juventus from Leeds for a British record fee.

Having left behind a world of maximum wages pegged at £20-a-week in England the handsome Welshman knew he could enjoy wealth beyond compare in Italy.

The hero of Elland Road became a superstar at Juventus. In fact, he was so good for them that at their club's centenary in 1997 Juve fans voted Charles the best import their club had ever signed. He scored 93 goals in 155 matches for Juve and in many of those games he was playing at centre-half.

FOOTBALL STAR IS SOLD for £70,000

By FRANK McGHEE

JOHN CHARLES, the 6ft. 2in., twenty-five-year-old Leeds United centre forward, is to join an Italian club for the highest-ever transfer fee in British Soccer —about £70,000.

The deal between Leeds United and Juventus —of Turin—was completed yesterday.

About £60,000 of the fee will go to Leeds United, the rest to Charles, who is a Welsh International.

Charles's pretty wife Peggy, who is expecting her third baby any day now, said last night: "It feels like winning the pools. But wherever we go I shall look after the children myself.

Free Car

"What I should really like is somebody to do the other work—nappies and things. We shall NOT stay in Italy indefinitely. We want the children to be educated in Britain."

If Charles had moved to another British club he would have received the usual signing-on fee of £10. Apart from the lump sum of £10,000, Charles will earn up to £80 a week playing for Juventus. Maximum weekly wage in British Soccer is £15.

Charles will also have a flat in Turin and a car —provided free by Juventus.

His contract will be for two years. After that he will be able to negotiate another contract—with the chance of getting even better terms.

In British Soccer the contract a player signs with his club has no fixed time limit.

Charles, known to Soccer fans as "King John" and "Charles the Great," plays his last game on Leeds United's home ground on Monday against Sunderland.

He is due to leave for Turin on Tuesday to choose his flat.

Charles will join Juventus after Leeds United's tour of Holland next month.

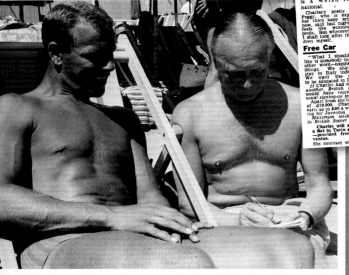

Never Go Back

Don Revie persuaded the Leeds board to bring King John back in 1962 but it was a move that did not pay off. Charles could not recapture the form that made him the Leeds hero of the Fifties. He was hampered by injuries and fitness issues and made just 11 appearances before heading back to Serie A with Roma.

The Man Who Made Leeds

Revie in action as Leeds player.

restricted transfers. He goes straight into Fulham's League side against West Ham.

"My only worry now is the responsibility of helping Fulham stay in the First Division," Dodgin added.

DON REVIE, became manager of struggling Leeds United yesterday. He succeeded Jack Taylor, who resigned this week.

Revie will continue to play for Leeds.

"He is being given the full title, not 'player-manager'," said chairman Sam Bolton.

DEREK DOUGLAS, Blackburn centre forward, flew back from Belgium and said he is not yet prepared to sign for Anderlecht.

Trainer Doug Davidson and Peter Harris, former England right winger, have applied for the vacant PORTSMOUTH managership.

Don had enjoyed the taste of glory. He devised the Revie Plan for a deep-lying striker during his days with Manchester City. He was voted the Footballer of the Year in 1955 and won the FA Cup with City, and colleague Bert Trautmann, in 1956.

Don Revie meets young fans at Wembley.

Don Revie wins Manager of the Year in 1969.

Daylight Robbery

Johnny Giles was the ultimate midfield maestro. The Republic of Ireland international was a brilliant reader of the game who was blessed with sublime technical skills. He could also sense the mood of a match and affect it with his pinpoint passing, his awareness of frailties in the opposition defence and a ruthless streak in his tackling that made him one of the most feared opponents of his generation. Given the years of impressive service he delivered for Leeds it's amazing to think he cost just £33,000 when recruited from Manchester United after being in their 1963 FA Cup-winning team.

At the time Giles was just 22, and many people wondered why the Old Trafford club were prepared to sell such a gifted young player. Giles had always been opinionated. He believes his outspoken views proved his downfall with manager Matt Busby at Old Trafford. In Leeds boss Don Revie he found a sporting soulmate: a manager willing to provide him with the kind of midfield stage and the belief he craved.

Giles left the FA Cup winners and a Division One club to move to Leeds, a team struggling in the lower reaches of Division Two. It was an inspired move for Leeds and Giles.

Giles relished the organization Revie brought to the club. After a slow start he emerged as a key player for the upwardly mobile Yorkshire club. And if a combination of Giles, Bobby Collins and Billy Bremner was not the tallest midfield unit in football, there was no disguising their skill, determination and commitment.

> **Selling Johnny to Leeds, not seeing his potential as a midfield player, was my greatest mistake in football.**
>
> Sir Matt Busby

FOOTBALL
–STATS–
Johnny Giles

Name: Michael John Giles

Date of birth: 6th November 1940

Place of birth: Dublin, Republic of Ireland

Position: Midfield

Leeds career: 1963–75

Leeds appearances: 525

Leeds goals: 115

Republic of Ireland: 59 caps, 5 goals

Revie signing Johnny Giles from Man Utd.

> *During the Sixties it was a tough game.*
> *My attitude was that if I was going to make a living*
> *I'm going to have to be as tough as everyone else.*
>
> Johnny Giles

> *I can't say I was an angel but I don't apologize for that.*
>
> Bobby Collins

Dirty Leeds

If one player's recruitment is acknowledged as the inspiration behind the Revie glory years it has to be the arrival of the diminutive Scotsman, Bobby Collins.

He was a 31-year-old cast off by Everton when he joined a Leeds team that was looking more likely to end up in Division Three than emerge as one of the most powerful clubs in England within three years.

Collins was 5ft 3in tall, wore size four boots and weighed around 10 stone. When you met Bobby it was hard to believe that the affable, smiling Scotsman was the same person as the tough, tenacious and very talented midfield general who skippered Leeds out of Division Two and ensured they competed at the top of Division One while also reaching the 1965 FA Cup final. He'd been ditched by Scotland six years earlier but his form for Leeds forced his recall.

And in 1965, after a season that saw Leeds finish as runners-up in both Division One and the FA Cup, Collins was named as the Footballer of the Year. This was the first time the award had ever been handed to a Leeds player.

Over the next five years that honour would be handed to Jack Charlton and Billy Bremner. Collins, who cost just £25,000, was the foundation stone that the astute Revie built his vibrant young team around. The exciting potential of his team-mates proved an inspiration to Collins. Revie's Leeds and Bobby Collins were made for one another.

Johnny Giles said: "Bobby was the most inspiring captain, a true general. During a match his voice could be heard all over the pitch, shouting encouragement and advice, or cursing and cajoling anyone who wasn't performing."

He became part of the football vernacular, as managers and pundits would say a club needed "an experienced man to do a Bobby Collins for them". It was a nice idea. Few, if any, could emulate the little Scotsman.

Before The Storm

Skippers Bobby Collins (left) and Denis Law shake hands before the 1965 FA Cup semi-final between Leeds and Manchester United at Hillsborough. The smiles were short-lived.

> " *I want Leeds United to attain the status which Manchester United enjoy in the world.*
>
> Don Revie "

The Battle Of Hillsborough

There was no doubting the ferocious rivalry between Leeds and Manchester United. Their first FA Cup semi-final clash at Hillsborough in 1965 stunned many observers. International team-mates piled into each other. Jack Charlton almost ripped Denis Law's shirt off his back. Many years later, when Jack and Denis met up, there was no disguising the old warriors' deep-rooted affection for each other (right).

Bobby Collins (left) and Billy Bremner hear the news that Bremner has been cleared by the FA disciplinary department to play in the 1965 Cup final.

History Beckons

The 1965 FA Cup final against Liverpool was Leeds United's first ever Wembley appearance. It also proved a historic moment for their South African winger Albert Johanneson. He became the first black player to appear in a Cup final. Albert was a brilliantly gifted winger. However, he combined exquisite skills and blistering pace with a frustrating degree of inconsistency. Like the rest of his team-mates he had an off-day at Wembley. Leeds lost 2-1 with all the goals coming in extra time.

Billy Bremner lies on the pitch while Liverpool's Tommy Smith (right) protests his innocence.

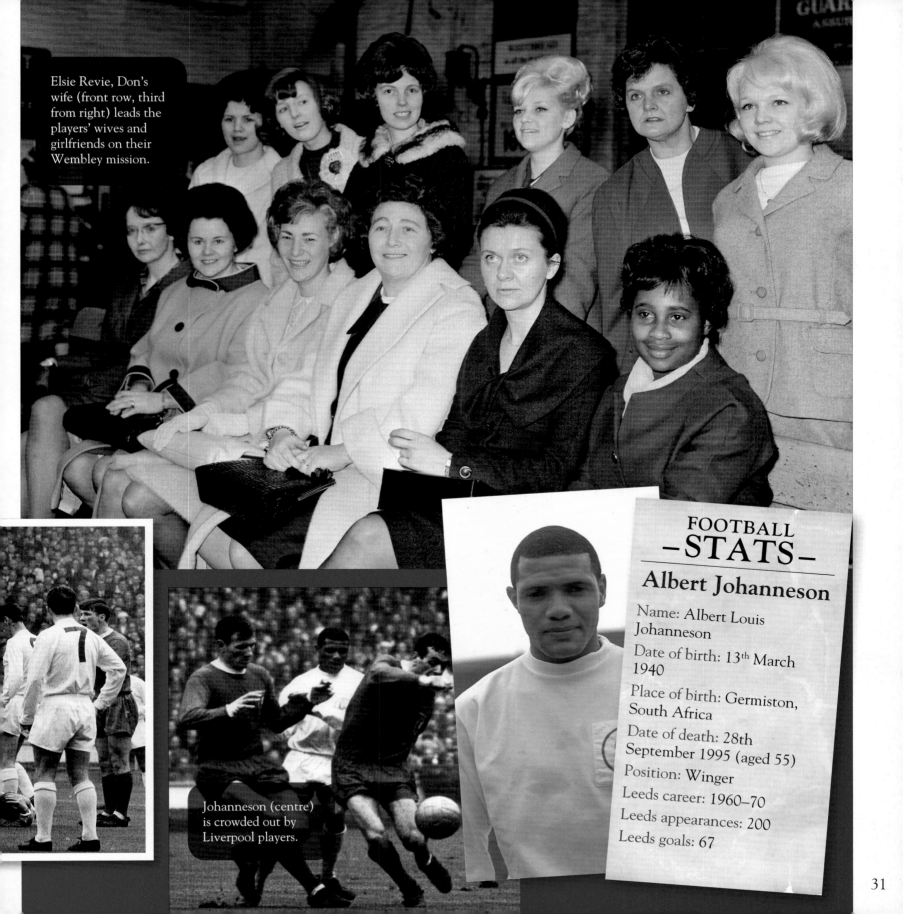

Elsie Revie, Don's wife (front row, third from right) leads the players' wives and girlfriends on their Wembley mission.

Johanneson (centre) is crowded out by Liverpool players.

FOOTBALL
—STATS—
Albert Johanneson

Name: Albert Louis Johanneson

Date of birth: 13th March 1940

Place of birth: Germiston, South Africa

Date of death: 28th September 1995 (aged 55)

Position: Winger

Leeds career: 1960–70

Leeds appearances: 200

Leeds goals: 67

Back To The Classroom

> "Don Revie brought a knowledge to the game which I don't think anybody has ever come close to. I played under Matt Busby, who was an old-fashioned type of manager, whose method was to get good players in, believe in them and let them go out and play. But Matt was never on the training ground, whereas Don was out there every day. If we lost a goal on Saturday, he'd be there, working out what happened and who was at fault. And he'd put it right."

Johnny Giles

Don Revie never disguised his quest for learning in football. He was also willing to help budding young managers. Two of the most respected managers of the Sixties were John Harris, of Sheffield United, and Barnsley's Johnny Steele. Together with Don Revie, they were the football professors to a group of keen managers-in-waiting at a FA teach-in at Leeds University in 1969. Huddersfield Town boss Ian Greaves was already making his mark. And in the class, on the third row, you'll see future England boss Graham Taylor.

Jack Charlton and Bobby Collins.

Revie with Syd Owen and Ian Greaves.

Members of the class – Graham Taylor on third row.

Revie (centre) with Sheffield United manager John Harris (left) and Barnsley boss Johnny Steele.

Don's Family Fortunes

Don Revie prided himself on making Leeds United an extension of his family. There was even a joke within the dressing room when the manager challenged players to a round of golf. Invariably Don would play with Norman Hunter and say to his young defender: "Come on son, we'll take them on." When the manager had left the room there were plenty of wisecracks for Norman to withstand for being the son of Don.

> "Don Revie created a family atmosphere at the club. He cared about us all. You have to have great team spirit. It was instilled into us as young boys. That was a big reason for our success.
>
> Billy Bremner"

ABOVE: (From left) Alan Peacock, Johnny Giles, Paul Madeley and Norman Hunter line up a putt.

RIGHT: Revie playing golf.

BELOW: Players and their families visit Harewood House to meet the club's new owl mascot, accompanied by Lady Harewood whose husband was Leeds United president.

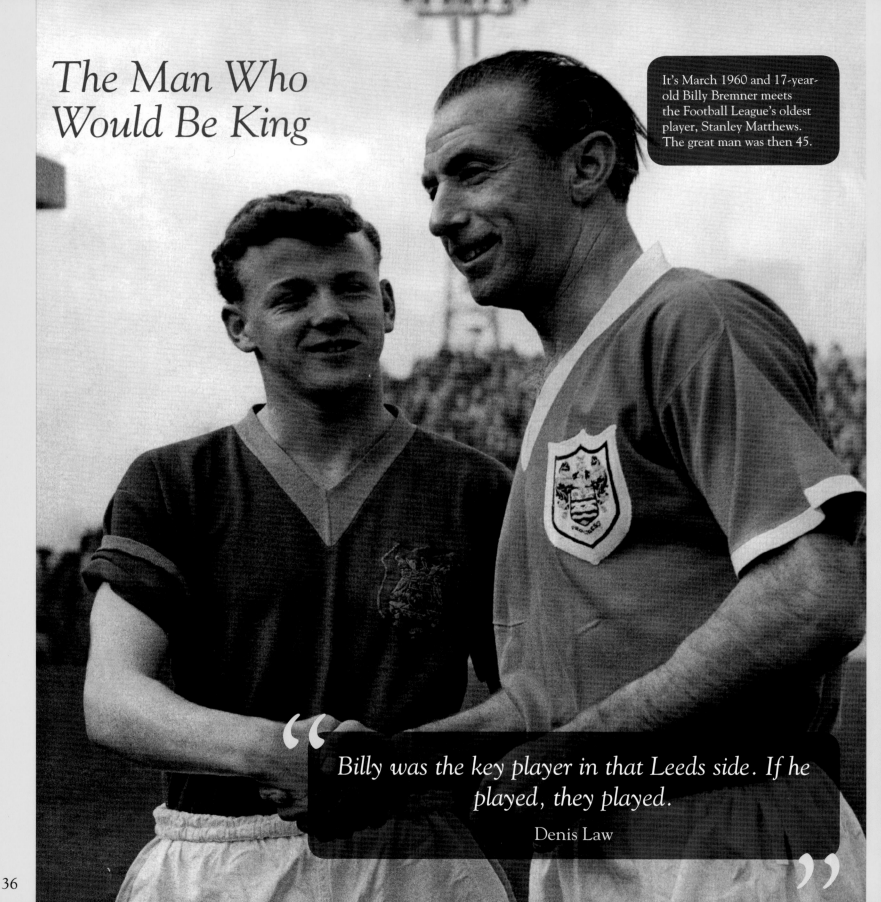

The Man Who Would Be King

It's March 1960 and 17-year-old Billy Bremner meets the Football League's oldest player, Stanley Matthews. The great man was then 45.

> "Billy was the key player in that Leeds side. If he played, they played.
>
> Denis Law"

It's hardly conceivable that the flame-haired teenager making the grade as a winger with a Division Two club would go on to become one of the all-time greats. Billy Bremner was switched from the right wing into a central role. He revelled in it and became an inspirational skipper of Leeds and Scotland.

"
Billy Bremner was a fireball. How I would have liked to have a man of his ability and inspiration in my side. He was splendid at improvising play and was a leader to inspire men.

Pelé
"

FOOTBALL –STATS–

Billy Bremner

Name: William (Billy) John Bremner

Date of birth: 9th December 1942

Place of birth: Stirling, Scotland

Date of death: 7th December 1997 (aged 54)

Position: Midfield

Leeds career: 1959–76

Leeds appearances: 772

Leeds goals: 115

Scotland: 54 caps, 3 goals

"Ten Stones Of Barbed Wire"

Bremner fighting Mike England.

> " He was fearless. He was 5 feet 5 ins tall and would take on giant centre-backs like Liverpool's Ron Yeats, who was 6 ft 4 ins. He was tenacious and one of his great attributes was that he never knew when he was beaten. "
>
> Peter Lorimer

> " Yes Billy had a temper but he also had immense ability. Billy had great heart, great enthusiasm and great fighting spirit. He also had great feet, great perception of passing and an ability to score match-winning goals. What a player. "
>
> Sir Alex Ferguson

If one man epitomised the skill, spirit and tenacity of the Leeds United revolution it was Billy Bremner.

In a famous newspaper article he was described as "ten stones of barbed wire." The aggressive, combative side to Billy's game was always there. After all, he was a winner and totally committed to his team's cause.

But the people who derided his skills did the red-headed genius from Stirling a massive disservice. It was Bob Paisley, Liverpool's legendary manager, who broke down the attributes required of midfielders into four categories. They had to win the ball, cover vast distances, pass the ball with accuracy and score goals. Paisley said: "You can count the players who can do this on one hand. They're a rarity. Billy Bremner was one of that priceless group."

He did cite Graeme Souness and Bryan Robson as others but even the skippers of Liverpool and Manchester United could not match Bremner's ability to score goals in the biggest, most testing matches.

Billy Bremner was unique.

Bremner celebrates.

39

At Home With The Bremners

Billy Bremner and his son in front of a George Best poster.

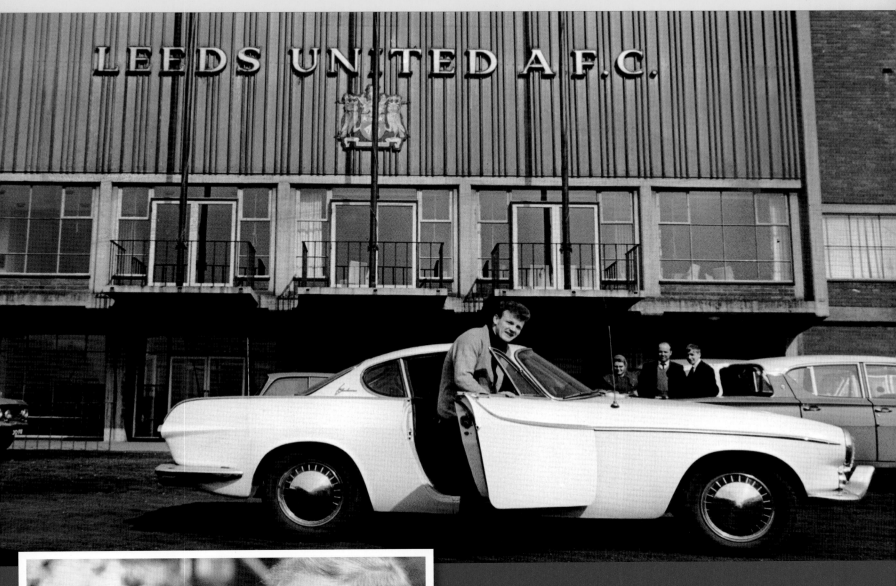

ABOVE: In the Sixties the white Volvo P1800 sports car was synonymous with Simon Templar, the star character of the popular TV programme *The Saint*. Billy may have been no saint but he did have a white Volvo sports car!

LEFT: Bremner was the third Leeds old boy in succession challenged to restore the club to greatness. He came the closest. But the bitter disappointment of losing the FA Cup semi-final to Coventry became real heartbreak when Leeds lost the first ever promotion play-off final to Charlton after a replay in 1987.

Billy firmly believed he was the best midfielder in the world. It turned out he probably was.

Mick Bates

Don Revie got a lot of great players together and got them to love the club, to play for each other and Billy was his right-hand man on the park. He was fiercely competitive but he was also a funny man. He could make you laugh with his wit and banter. He also let you know if you were letting the side down.

Eddie Gray

43

Midget Gems

Down the years two signings have been acknowledged as the inspirations behind Leeds United glory days. The first was Bobby Collins. The second was Gordon Strachan. Both were Scotland internationals leaving top-flight clubs to move to Division Two Leeds. Having turned 30, some people thought their days at the top were over. To Collins and Strachan the move to Leeds provided them with the perfect opportunity to prove their critics wrong.

Both skippered Leeds to promotion as Division Two champions, then inspired their team-mates to ensure the progress continued in the top flight. Strachan was the skipper when Leeds won the League Championship, the last time all 92 clubs were involved, in 1992.

Both were great team men. Both were deservedly awarded with one of the game's greatest individual honours, when they were voted Footballer of the Year: Collins in 1965, Strachan in 1991.

Howard Wilkinson, the manager who signed Strachan for Leeds from Manchester United for £300,000, reflected: "I've worked with some truly influential players but never one to match the part Gordon played in my career, and the development of Leeds. Cast off by Manchester United, there were times when he carried our team on his shoulders and made sure we fulfilled our ambitions. At the age of 35 and two months Gordon was the captain of Leeds who stepped forward to collect the League Championship trophy. It must have been a moment of great pride for him and his family."

FOOTBALL –STATS–

Gordon Strachan

Name: Gordon David Strachan OBE

Date of birth: 9th February 1957

Place of birth: Edinburgh, Scotland

Position: Midfield

Leeds career: 1989–95

Leeds appearances: 244

Leeds goals: 43

Scotland: 50 caps, 5 goals

Footballer of the Year

1965: Bobby Collins

1970: Billy Bremner

1991: Gordon Strachan

Come On You Whites

October 1968 *Leeds United 3 Standard Liège 2.*

Don Revie had promised to attack in the first leg in Belgium but United had to be content with a goalless draw.

The second leg at Elland Road kicked off late after a controversial warm-up. United had already been waiting for Standard Liège for five minutes and were stunned when they finally appeared in an all-white kit, sparking 15 minutes of heated argument.

Standard's normal strip was red shirts and white shorts, which they had worn in Belgium. For some strange reason they chose to arrive in England with only an all-white kit, even though they knew they would spark a colour clash.

Billy Bremner pointed out the problem to referee Gunnar Michaelsen, who asked Standard to change strip. With Don Revie and Standard coach Roger Petit arguing bitterly in the tunnel about who should change, matters became farcical.

The Belgians argued that they only had the white kit with them and that the rules made it clear that the onus was on the home team to change. United accepted the point, but asserted that Standard had caused the problem by their strange choice of kit.

United's change strip of all blue was offered to the Belgians, but they claimed angrily that it did not fit and blatantly ignored the officials' decree that they should change.

Leeds finally broke the deadlock by playing, and winning, in blue.

Coach Syd Owen made sure the problem couldn't arise again when Napoli were the visitors to Elland Road. He checked that they had their own blue kit.

VISITING TEAM

46

Nice Day For A White Wedding

The squad turned out in numbers for the weddings of Paul Reaney (right) and Terry Copper (below). And the only people wearing all white were the wives.

Hard Men?
We're Having
A Laugh

Vinnie Jones in the gym.

David Batty.

Norman Hunter.

> " Batts possessed the tenacity of a terrier but inside that aggressive shell was a real talent. His technique at volleys and half-volleys and in passing the long ball long and short was impressive. "
>
> Howard Wilkinson

49

The emergence of David Batty was saluted by every Leeds United fan. They had grown-up on homegrown talent, many of them local boys, making the grade to the first team.

Their club might be stuck in Division Two but Batts, as everybody knew him, epitomised the hope of a brighter tomorrow. Leeds United clearly meant more to this son of a local dustbin man. There was a touch of devil in his tackling yet he possessed great skills and an ability to read the game.

There could only ever be one Billy Bremner. But in his early days the embryo Batty gained some genuine comparisons.

Vinnie's Warm-Up

Pick on somebody your own size, Vinnie.

" Some said he couldn't pass water and that with every attempted pass he committed GBH on the football. I sensed that inside that shaven, glowering, hard man's head a footballer was trying to get out. "

Howard Wilkinson on Vinnie Jones

Vinnie celebrates scoring a goal.

It must rank as the most controversial recruitment in Leeds United's modern history. When it was announced in 1989 that Leeds were paying Wimbledon £650,000 for midfield hard man Vinnie Jones many critics of the club just revived their old put down: "Dirty Leeds." But manager Howard Wilkinson believed the former hod carrier could play a crucial role in United's bid to return to the top flight. Wilkinson explained: "Vinnie was a man with the self-confidence, assertiveness and downright ego to operate in the pressure cooker atmosphere that would be part of Leeds' season. "I also thought Vinny could help Gordon Strachan to galvanize the team without ever undermining the old man's status as our captain and senior professional. For a notorious bad boy to be cautioned just twice in a season with Leeds was not a bad record and, overall, he proved to be the man for the job."

Jones became an Elland Road hero. He only made 46 appearances for the club before moving on to Sheffield United, but he fulfilled the challenge of playing a role in the club's promotion push. He had the club's crest tattooed on his leg as a permanent reminder of the Division Two championship campaign of 1989–90. To this day Leeds fans, especially members of the Leeds United Disabled Organization, speak fondly of the time and energy Vinnie put into his commitment to them.

So Close To Disaster

Leeds v Sunderland, FA Cup fifth-round replay, 15th March 1967.   Elland Road's record attendance: 57,892.

It's fair to say that in the Sixties one of the bitterest rivalries in English football lay between Leeds and Sunderland. The normal rules of combat were observed when they met in the FA Cup in 1965. The first game at Roker Park ended 1-1 and included a string of wild challenges and a feud between Sunderland's Jim Baxter and United's Johnny Giles.

Leeds didn't have time to make the replay, four days later, all-ticket. And while the game was not as explosive on the field, there was almost a tragedy off it. A record attendance of 57,892 – about 5,000 above normal capacity – packed into Elland Road, with thousands more locked outside. Some spectators claimed the attendance was nearer 60,000, such was the widespread overcrowding.

Chairman Harry Reynolds had vowed over the previous couple of seasons to revamp Elland Road and make it one of the best grounds in the country. So there was shock around the stadium when the events in the Lowfields Road terracing developed.

Steel and concrete crush barriers collapsed under the pressure of the packed terracing. It was estimated that about 1,000 fans had to escape the crush by invading the pitch in a human flood. Thankfully, there were no perimeter fences to block their escape. A police officer dashed onto the pitch to ask the referee to stop the game and the players went off as police and ambulance men dashed across with stretchers.

Geoffrey Green, in *The Times*, wrote: "It looked like a battlefield. Girls were hysterical and ambulances could not get near the ground for some of the crowds and traffic held up outside."

It could have been a disaster. Thankfully, nobody was killed and only 32 people were taken to hospital for treatment. After a 17-minute break the game resumed and Leeds ran out, 1-0 winners.

Boys On Tour

From left, David Harvey, Johnny Giles, Mick Jones and Terry Hibbitt arrive in Manchester on their way to the airport and a flight to Budapest.

There was a huge novelty factor when Leeds launched their foreign sorties in the Sixties and Seventies. Not too many people ventured so far afield. A Leeds director gave the game away when the club were drawn to play Standard Liège of Belgium. He said: "I'm looking forward to this trip. I've never been to Standard before!"

ABOVE: Quite what Paul Reaney and David Harvey's wives made of their purchases on the trip for the 1973 Cup Winners' Cup final in Thessalonica remains unknown.

RIGHT: Billy Bremner (left) sports a natty trilby on returning from Valencia with Mike O'Grady and Jim Storrie.

*That Winning
Feeling… At Last*

1968: *The first trophy*
SCORE: *Arsenal 0 Leeds United 1 (Cooper)*

Players' reception.

TOP LEFT: Gary Sprake (left) and Terry Cooper parade the cup.

ABOVE: (From left) Gary Sprake, Paul Reaney, Billy Bremner, Peter Lorimer, Johnny Giles and Terry Cooper salute the Leeds fans.

LEFT: Bremner holds up the cup

BELOW: Leeds fans celebrate.

Big Jack's Hat-Trick

"
I was a one-man awkward squad. One day Don Revie told me: 'If I were a manager I wouldn't have you in my team.' Thankfully he wasn't the manager then. He was a Leeds player.

Jack Charlton
"

Jack Charlton wins an aerial duel with Sheffield Wednesday's Don Megson in the 1-1 FA Cup third-round tie at Hillsborough, January 1969.

FOOTBALL –STATS–

Jack Charlton

NAME: John (Jack) Charlton OBE

Date of birth: 8th May 1935

Place of birth: Ashington

Position: Centre-back

Leeds career: 1952–73

Leeds appearances: 773

Leeds goals: 95

England: 35 caps, 6 goals

ABOVE: Jack in a Household Cavalry outfit.

LEFT: Jack in a bowler.

61

England
UNITED

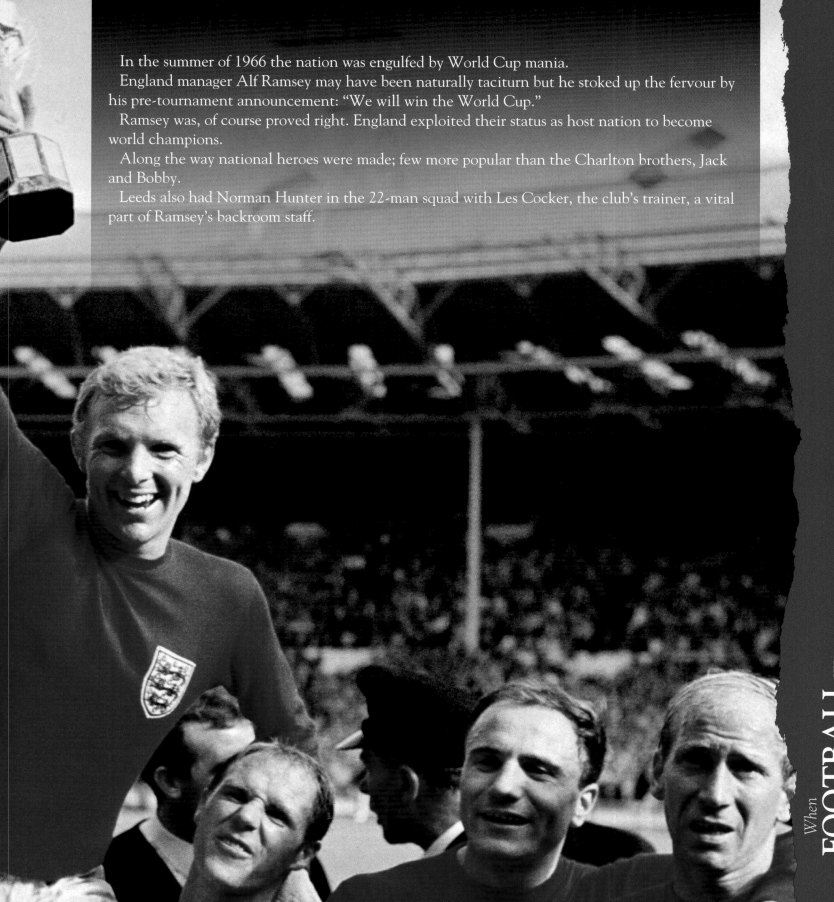

In the summer of 1966 the nation was engulfed by World Cup mania.

England manager Alf Ramsey may have been naturally taciturn but he stoked up the fervour by his pre-tournament announcement: "We will win the World Cup."

Ramsey was, of course proved right. England exploited their status as host nation to become world champions.

Along the way national heroes were made; few more popular than the Charlton brothers, Jack and Bobby.

Leeds also had Norman Hunter in the 22-man squad with Les Cocker, the club's trainer, a vital part of Ramsey's backroom staff.

1949–50 Buckley unveils a younger team finishing fifth in the Second Division. **1952–53** John Charles switches from centre-back to centre-forward and scores 27 goals in 29 appearances. Leeds finish 10th. Buckley resigns. **1953–54** Raich Carter is the new manager. Leeds again finish 10th. **1955–56** Leeds win promotion as runners-up in Division Two. **1956–57** Leeds finish eighth in the top flight. In September 1956 a fire destroys the West Stand at Elland Road. Damage of £100,000 and the club is under-insured. To help pay for the new stand John Charles sold to Juventus for £65,000 – a world-record fee. **1957–58** Leeds finish 17th. Carter's contract is not renewed. **1958–59** Bill Lambton takes over as acting manager. In January Lambton sacked and Willis Edwards returns as manager. Lambton's legacy is signing England international Don Revie. **1959–60** Jack Taylor made manager. The season ends in relegation and Taylor resigns in March 1961 to be replaced by new manager Revie. **1961–62** Revie bolsters team with the £25,000 club record signing – Bobby Collins from Everton. In the last game of the season at Newcastle a victory is needed to avoid relegation – Leeds win 3-0. **1962–63** John Charles is bought back from Juventus in August for £53,000. Revie introduces talented home-grown youngsters. **1963–64** Johnny Giles arrives from Manchester United for £33,000. Leeds are Second Division champions. **1964–65** Leeds finish runners-up to Manchester United on goal difference and lose FA Cup final 2-1 to Liverpool; Albert Johanneson becomes the first black player to play in an FA Cup final. Bobby Collins is Footballer of the Year. **1965–66** Leeds runners-up again and reach the semi-finals of the Inter-Cities Fairs Cup. **1966–67** Billy Bremner is confirmed as Leeds' captain. The FA Cup fifth-round replay against Sunderland creates the record attendance at Elland Road – 57,892, around 5,000 above the stadium's normal capacity. Reach the final of the Inter-Cities Fairs Cup, but lose 2-0 in the away leg to Dinamo Zagreb and draw at home 0-0. Jack Charlton is Footballer of the Year. **1967–68** Record signing, centre-forward Mick Jones from Sheffield United for £100,000. Leeds finally win a trophy beating Arsenal in the League Cup. They lose the FA Cup semi to Everton and become the first British club to win the Fairs Cup beating Ferencvaros. Finish fourth in the League. **1968–69** Leeds win the First Division title. **1969–70** Leeds chase an historic treble of League title, FA Cup and European Cup. Forced to play eight games in 14 days. Club loose the European semi-final to Celtic and loose an FA Cup final replay to Chelsea to end season without a trophy.

Jack Becomes A National Hero

Jack was a late developer but when he matured he became the best centre-back in the country. The two men who helped him fulfil his undoubted talent were Don Revie and England boss Sir Alf Ramsey. Here, Jack's relaxing at the England team's hotel during the 1966 World Cup finals.

Big Jack And Wor Bob *England's Favourite Family*

The Charlton brothers were hailed as conquering heroes wherever they went after England won the World Cup in 1966. They were stunned by the reception they received on returning for a civic reception in their home town of Ashington, Northumberland.

In 1994, when Bobby was knighted for his services to football, Jack said: "I'm thrilled for our kid but he'll always be wor Bob to me."

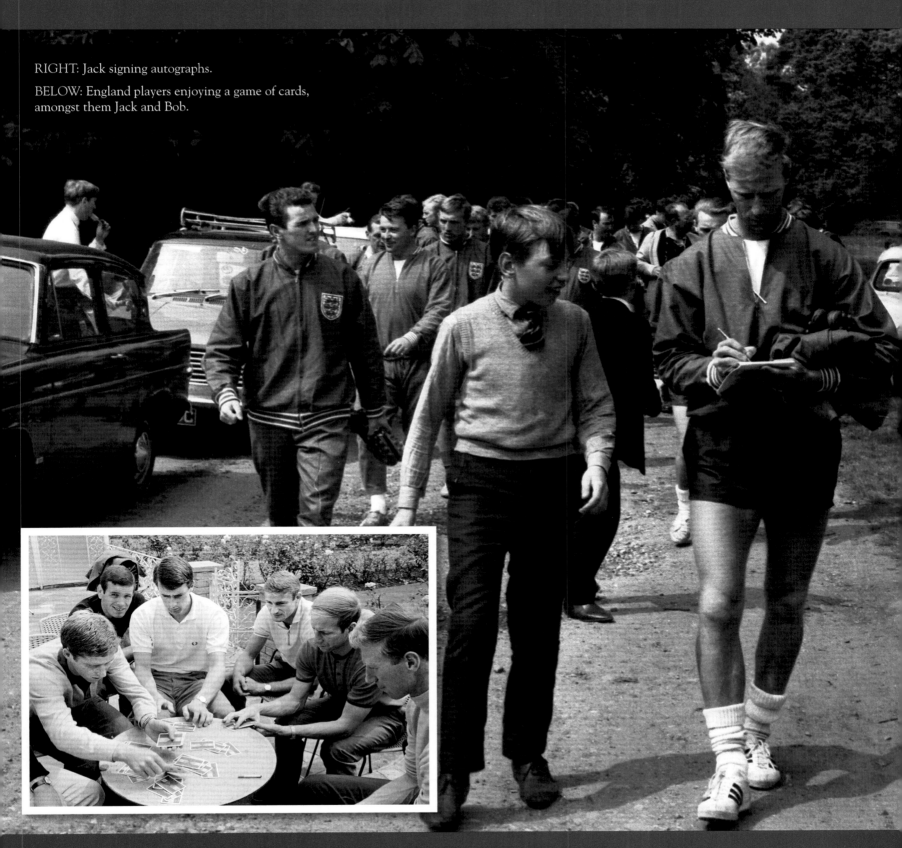

RIGHT: Jack signing autographs.

BELOW: England players enjoying a game of cards, amongst them Jack and Bob.

Fit To Be Kings

The squad for the 1968–69 campaign that saw Leeds emerge as Division One champions for the first time in the club's history. They collected a record points total and only three players had cost a fee in transfers.

> We clinched the title with a 0-0 draw at Liverpool. We had finally done it. We were champions. 'Go down to the Kop end,' Don said. We were a bit tentative at first but Don was right. 'Champions! Champions!' the Kop chanted. It was a fabulous moment.
>
> Johnny Giles

Revie and his backroom staff.

Revie wins Manager of the Year in 1969.

Jonah And The Wails

Don Revie paid a club record fee of £100,000 to recruit Mick Jones from Sheffield United in 1967. Jones was a brave, selfless and tireless centre-forward. He fitted into the United scheme of things immediately and, while he was Cup-tied and couldn't help Leeds win their breakthrough trophy in 1968, there was no doubting the role he would play over the next few years.

The arrival of Allan Clarke from Leicester City a couple of years later put together one of the most lethal and dynamic goal-scoring partnerships seen in English football in the last 50 years. Clarke may have had the more clinical touch but Jones played his part with his physical commitment and never-say-die attitude. They were a pair of strikers made for each other.

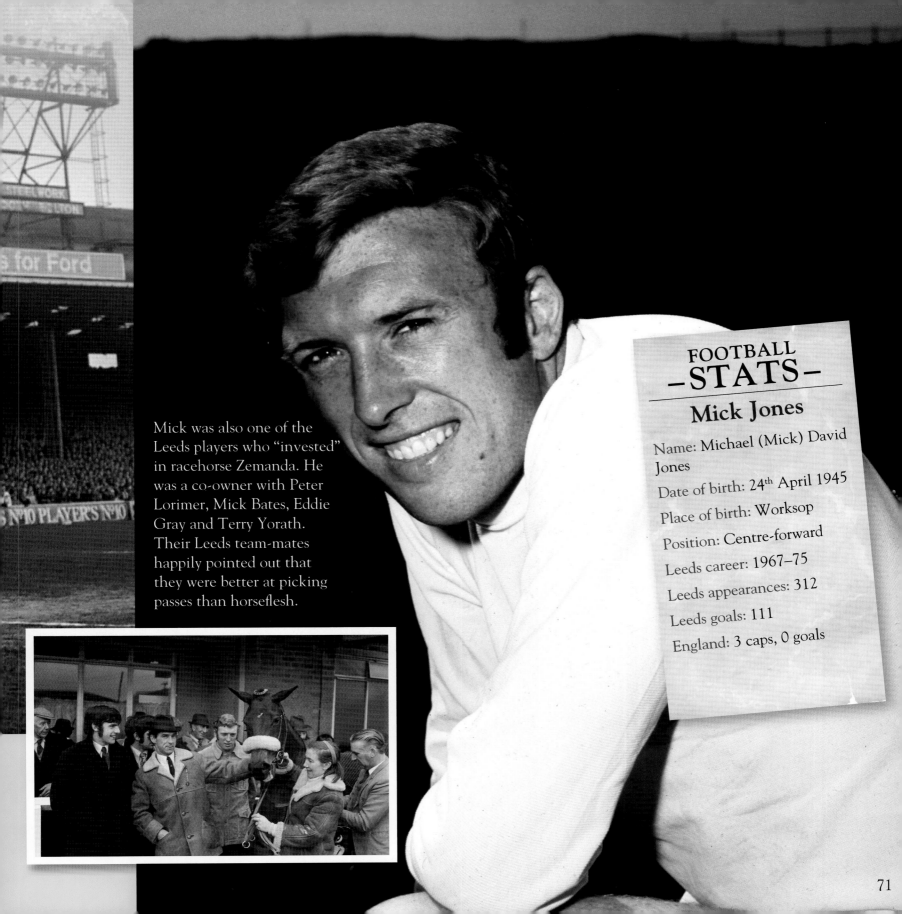

Mick was also one of the Leeds players who "invested" in racehorse Zemanda. He was a co-owner with Peter Lorimer, Mick Bates, Eddie Gray and Terry Yorath. Their Leeds team-mates happily pointed out that they were better at picking passes than horseflesh.

FOOTBALL –STATS–

Mick Jones

Name: Michael (Mick) David Jones

Date of birth: 24th April 1945

Place of birth: Worksop

Position: Centre-forward

Leeds career: 1967–75

Leeds appearances: 312

Leeds goals: 111

England: 3 caps, 0 goals

King Billy Hails Caesar

As the 1969–70 season reached its climax Leeds were on course for a stunning Treble.

They were trying to defend their League title, they marched into a European Cup semi-final against Celtic and they also reached the FA Cup final.

The fact that the domestic season had been shortened to allow England time to acclimatize for their World Cup defence in Mexico made fixture congestion a nightmare for Don Revie and his team. Sensing the demands were simply impossible, Leeds targeted the Cup competitions.

But they were beaten by Celtic in Europe and were left with the FA Cup final to focus on. In a one-sided first game they tore Chelsea apart, with Eddie Gray embarrassing the Blues' right-back David Webb. But with Gary Sprake letting in soft goals, Leeds couldn't protect their supremacy and the game ended 2-2.

Chelsea revamped their team for the replay at Old Trafford. Ron "Chopper" Harris was switched to right-back to deal with the threat of Eddie Gray. He achieved it by committing a wicked, late, knee-high tackle in the opening minutes that left Gray nursing an injury for the rest of the game. Later Harris admitted: "I could have been sent off for it but I got away with it and it helped us win the Cup."

Some of their fiercest critics branded Revie's Leeds as chokers after they ended the season empty-handed. The brutal reality was that being forced to play five critical games in eight days proved too much for them – and would have seen off any other club.

The Norman Invasion

> *Norman had a tremendous attitude. He was a truly great player. He read the game exceptionally well and was the best defender I ever played with.*
>
> Johnny Giles

FOOTBALL
–STATS–

Norman Hunter

Name: Norman Hunter

Date of birth: 29th October 1943

Place of birth: Gateshead

Position: Centre-back

Leeds career: 1962–76

Leeds appearances: 724

Leeds goals: 21

England: 28 caps, 2 goals

> *Norman must be one of the greatest players ever. He does not get full credit. Maybe the biggest tribute you could pay is this: Put him on the transfer list and everyone would want him.*
>
> Don Revie

Honest! Norman (centre) is the peacemaker in the 1974 Charity Shield bust-up.

Norman at home with wife Sue, baby Claire and son Michael in 1971.

Norman holds the PFA Player of the Year award in 1974 with his five-year-old son Michael.

So How Thorough Was Revie?

Leeds were drawn away to Sutton United, amateurs from the Isthmian League, in the FA Cup fourth round in 1970.

Typically, manager Don Revie was not going to allow a culture shock to derail his team. So he arranged for them to play a practice match on a local amateur side's January mud heap. It was all part of the preparations he felt would ensure that there would be no upset at Sutton.

The pre-match planning was impeccable. Leeds, who had everything to lose, ran out emphatic 6-0 winners.

> "Don was a visionary, he had ambition and in many aspects he was way ahead of his time. In terms of scouting the opposition, putting players on diets and bringing in rules like drinking no alcohol for at least 48 hours before a match… all those things were new to the game when Don introduced them, but everybody does it now.
>
> Peter Lorimer"

You Didn't Need That Lucky Suit, Don.

Don Revie had a lucky blue suit. He had worn it on match days for more than two years. The suit had been worn in Budapest when Leeds beat Ferencváros to win the Inter-Cities Fairs Cup. He'd worn it at Wembley for the 1968 League Cup victory over Arsenal and wherever Leeds played you'd see Don sporting his favourite blue suit.

But on the morning of an FA Cup third-round tie against Sheffield Wednesday at Elland Road in 1969, Don heard a tearing sound as he got dressed. The seam of his trousers had split. He switched to a grey suit and Wednesday won 3-1.

At the time Don admitted: "Sure I'm superstitious – that's why I wore the lucky blue suit. Look what happened when it came apart."

Superstition did, of course, run through the club in the Revie years. For instance, Jack Charlton declined to be captain because he didn't want to lead the team out. He preferred to be the last man onto the field.

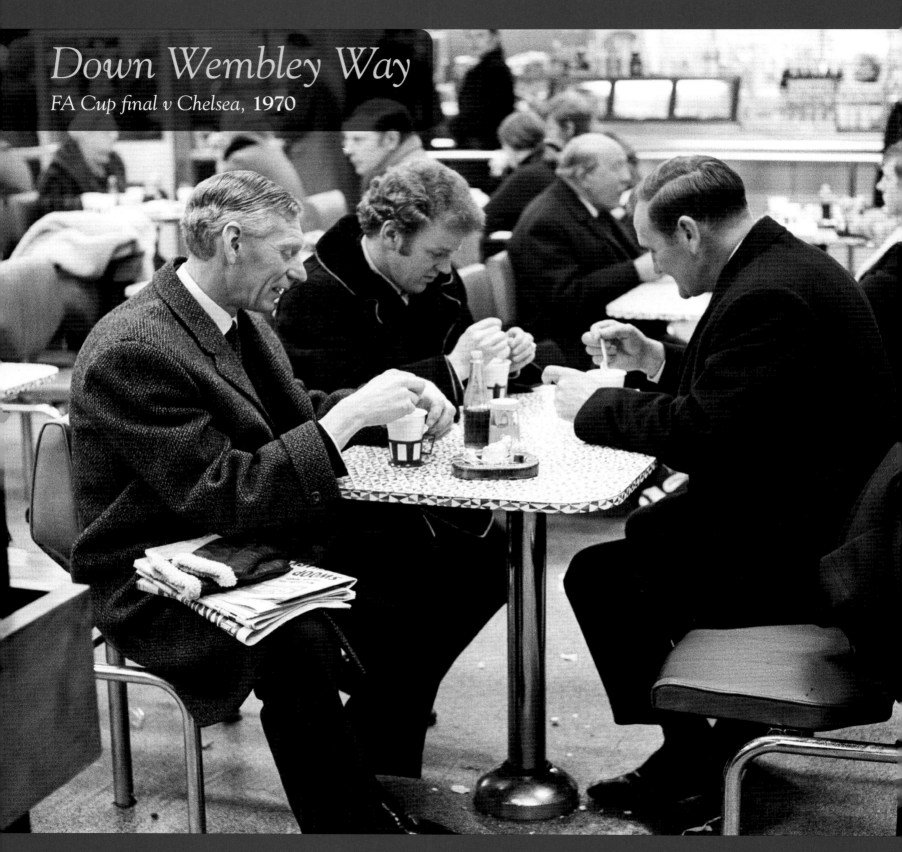

Boarding the train, Wembley bound.

Charlton's first goal.

In these days of VIP lounges and intense security it's remarkable to see the pictures of one of England's most famous football teams heading to London for the 1970 FA Cup final. Pictured left, skipper Billy Bremner sits with manager Don Revie and coach Syd Owen at the café at Leeds station. They're savouring their drinks surrounded by members of the public. There's no special treatment for the Leeds party. The table's made of Formica and the tomato ketchup is available if they want it.

Mick Jones scores Leeds' second goal.

The mood was mean whenever Leeds played Chelsea but on the heavy Wembley pitch there was at least one example of compassion to an old mate.

The pitch had been wrecked by the recent visit of the Horse of the Year show. Leeds defender Terry Cooper developed cramp and it was his England team-mate Peter Osgood who stopped to help his international colleague.

FOOTBALL -STATS-

Terry Cooper

Name: Terence (Terry) Cooper

Date of birth: 12th July 1944

Place of birth: Knottingley

Position: Left-back

Leeds career: 1962–75

Leeds appearances: 350

Leeds goals: 11

England: 20 caps, 0 goals

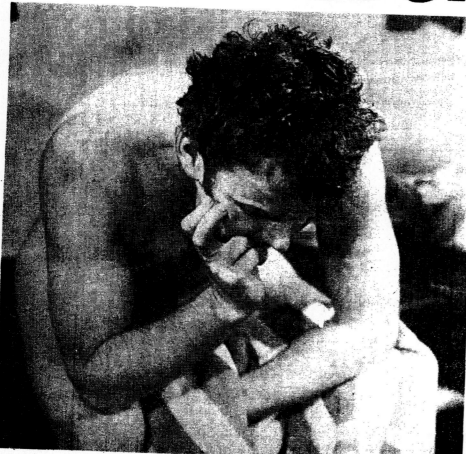

DAILY Mirror

6d. Thursday, April 30, 1970 ★★ No. 20,633

IT'S THE FINAL AGONY

..summed up in one picture

THIS is the picture that sums up the agony of it all.

Leeds United skipper Billy Bremner weeps in the Old Trafford dressing-rooms last night after his side's final disappointment in a season of bitter frustration.

The team that came so near to winning everything, finished up with nothing after Chelsea beat them 2—1 in the replayed F.A. Cup Final.

Once more the match went to extra time. Then a goal by Chelsea's David Webb sealed Leeds's fate.

It was the final blow in a season which has already seen the League championship and the European Cup snatched from their grasp.

Their players were so disappointed that they could not bear to take their place at the presentation of the losers' medals.

Sympathy

The medals were eventually presented to them in the dressing room by FA chairman Dr. Andrew Stephen.

For Leeds centre-half Jackie Charlton the price of his team's marathon effort could be even greater than their triple defeat.

Leeds manager Don Revie revealed after the game that Jackie had a pulled leg muscle that could keep him out of England's World Cup team.

Charlton said later: "The way my injury feels at the moment, I will not be going to Mexico".

Even the victorious Chelsea team had sympathy for defeated Leeds.

Said centre-half John Dempsey: "We feel very sorry for them and hope they do better next season".

Manager Revie said: "The lads are terribly disappointed. But we will start again next season and if we only have another one like this, I shan't be worried."

Four-page Cup Special Pull-Out inside. Round-up—Back Page.

Leeds have been stripped of their last chance of glory. And in the dressing room, skipper Billy Bremner weeps.

Picture by ALFRED MARKEY.

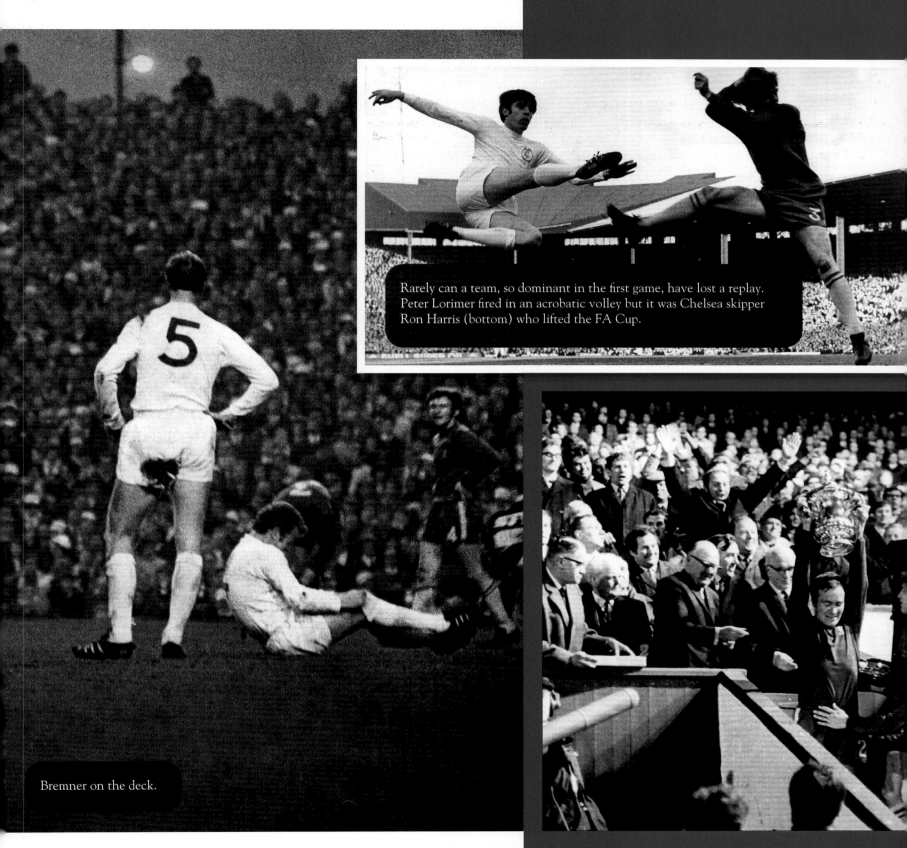

Rarely can a team, so dominant in the first game, have lost a replay. Peter Lorimer fired in an acrobatic volley but it was Chelsea skipper Ron Harris (bottom) who lifted the FA Cup.

Bremner on the deck.

The Title That Was Snatched Away

Leeds were top of the table and heading for the 1971 title when the most notorious offside decision not given undermined them. Referee Ray Tinkler, who had been lambasted for his ineffectiveness at previous games, was in charge.

West Bromwich Albion were the visitors and Jeff Astle the eventual scorer as Tinkler waved play on after a clear-cut offside decision was given against the visitors.

The scenes engulfing Elland Road were not pleasant as manager Don Revie remonstrated with the linesman who had flagged for the offside originally.

Players from both teams jostled the referee and the game was held up for five minutes. "The Leeds fans are going absolutely mad and they have every right to," commentator Barry Davies said on *Match of the Day*. There were 23 arrests.

West Brom won the match 2-1. Leeds won their last three games but finished the season one point behind the eventual champions, Arsenal.

And The Cup That Wasn't!

Leeds did have something to celebrate. And it looks as if Jack Charlton knows how.

They beat Juventus to lift the Inter-Cities Fairs Cup (later to be called the UEFA Cup).

Jeepers Keepers

Three goalies have featured in Leeds United's championship triumphs.

Gary Sprake, who had been in the team that reached Division One back in 1964, was the first choice throughout the Sixties. David Harvey, who was in the first team by 1974, had been Sprake's diligent and, at times, frustrated understudy.

And, by the time the 1992 title was won, John Lukic had been signed as a schoolboy by Leeds, sold to Arsenal for £75,000 and bought back as Leeds' first £1 million signing in 1990.

Lukic has a remarkable claim to fame in that he's the only goalie since the Second World War to win a League Championship medal with two clubs. He was the goalie on that famous night when Arsenal won 2-0 at Anfield to lift the title on goal difference.

Many critics believed that Don Revie's loyalty to Sprake cost Leeds trophies. Johnny Giles understands their logic. He said: "Don would ultimately admit he had a blind spot as far as Sprakey was concerned. David Harvey waited in the wings far too long, becoming frustrated, and mystified that he wasn't getting his chance."

FOOTBALL –STATS–

Gary Sprake

Name: Gary Sprake

Date of birth: 3rd April 1945

Place of birth: Swansea, Wales

Position: Goalkeeper

Leeds career: 1962–73

Leeds appearances: 506

Wales: 37 caps, 0 goals

Oops, Sprake lets a goal through his legs.

David Harvey

Name: David Harvey

Date of birth: 7th February 1948

Place of birth: Leeds

Position: Goalkeeper

Leeds career: 1965–80, 1980–81 and 1982–85

Leeds appearances: 446

Scotland: 16 caps, 0 goals

FOOTBALL
—STATS—

John Lukic

Name: Jovan (John) Lukic

Date of birth: 11th December 1960

Place of birth: Chesterfield

Position: Goalkeeper

Leeds career: 1978–83, 1990–96

Leeds appearances: 430

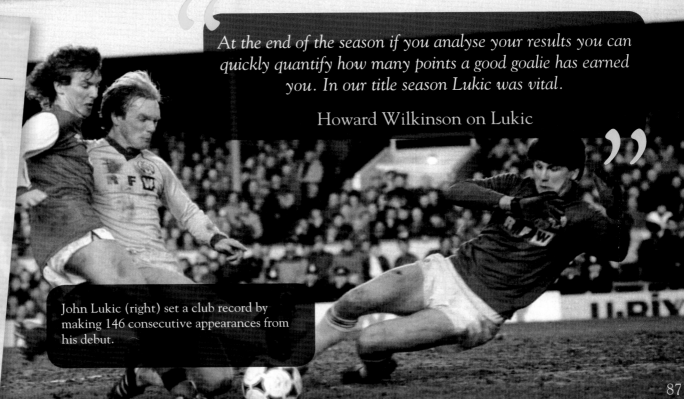

"
At the end of the season if you analyse your results you can quickly quantify how many points a good goalie has earned you. In our title season Lukic was vital.

Howard Wilkinson on Lukic
"

John Lukic (right) set a club record by making 146 consecutive appearances from his debut.

Careless Hands

It's a painful truth of the Revie team of the Sixties but one of
Don's few flaws was his loyalty to Gary Sprake.

There was no doubting Sprake's ability to produce
breathtaking saves. But on too many occasions he gifted soft
goals that left his team-mates staring in disbelief. Sprake was
haunted after throwing the ball into his own net at Liverpool.
The Kop fans taunted him by singing "Careless Hands".

Top That

In the spring of 1972 there was no disputing which club had the best, most honoured and most effective squad in football. Leeds United could boast 13 current full internationals: the 12 on show in the picture as well as England international left-back Terry Cooper. They had a domestic Double in their sights.

This was the squad that manager Don Revie challenged to win the one domestic trophy that had painfully eluded Leeds United – the FA Cup.

Tottenham were the FA Cup visitors as the Leeds team went through their pre-match drills.

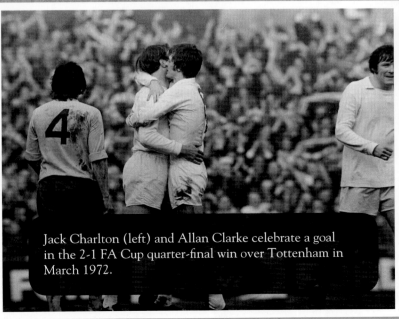

Jack Charlton (left) and Allan Clarke celebrate a goal in the 2-1 FA Cup quarter-final win over Tottenham in March 1972.

Johnny Giles(left) evades Birmingham's Alan Campbell in the 1972 FA Cup semi-final at Hillsborough. Leeds won 3-0.

100 Years Of FA Cup Finals

Revie and Bertie Mee lead out the teams.

Tommy Steele leads the singing.

It was the FA's attempt at pageantry. Her Majesty the Queen was in attendance to present the 1972 FA Cup to the winners of the Centenary final. The teams marched out through a guard of honour provided by the flags of all the clubs that had appeared in previous finals. It was a great spectacle.

Bremner and McLintock prepare for the coin toss.

Leeds Lift The Cup

Allan Clarke escapes Arsenal defender Peter Simpson.

Mick Jones soars above Frank McLintock.

Allan Clarke delivers a pinpoint, side-foot pass.

They were probably the most feared and effective double act in English football so there should have been no surprise when Mick Jones was the supplier and Allan Clarke the lethal finisher who ensured Leeds won the FA Cup for the first time in the club's history. Jones dislocated his elbow in the last minute of the game. Wracked with pain, he had to be helped up the steps to the Royal Box to collect his winner's medal by team-mate Norman Hunter. A League and Cup Double was now within their grasp. Leeds headed to Molineux on the Monday night, needing only a draw to ensure they were champions. For the past 18 months they had played some great football. Johnny Giles has recently reflected: "From Christmas of 1971 to the end of the 1972 season we produced our best football. At one point we were out of contention in the League. We went on to win the FA Cup and had the chance to win the title again on that Monday night."

Billy Bremner receives the FA Cup from Her Majesty the Queen.

Manager Don Revie (left) and his skipper and talisman, Billy Bremner.

The delighted players celebrate Leeds United's first ever FA Cup triumph.

Wives Christine Yorath (left) and Jill Bates look after the cup on the journey back to Leeds.

Don Revie and his players celebrate their historic triumph at the team's London reception.

The people of Leeds were ecstatic by their team's first ever FA Cup triumph. The fact that it was the Centenary final and that Arsenal, the previous season's Double winners, had been beaten made the taste of victory even sweeter.

In the years since then the status of the FA Cup has been severely undermined. A glimpse at the way the streets of Leeds as well as Elland Road stadium were packed for the homecoming of the Cup-winners eloquently emphasizes what it meant back then.

Don't Forget TC

There were many differences between Don Revie (above, in action as a player) and the man who was to succeed him in 1974, Brian Clough. One of them was their respective attitude to injured players. Terry Cooper, the Leeds and England left-back, had broken his leg a few weeks earlier. But there was no way Revie would allow the injured defender to slide out of the Wembley picture. Revie insisted on having his picture taken with Cooper and the cup in the aftermath of the 1972 final. Cooper was also wheeled around Elland Road by his team-mates when they returned to a civic reception in Leeds to mark the momentous occasion. Conversely, Clough preferred to keep away from injured players. His star men in later years believed this was linked to the fact his own career was cruelly cut short when he was just 27.

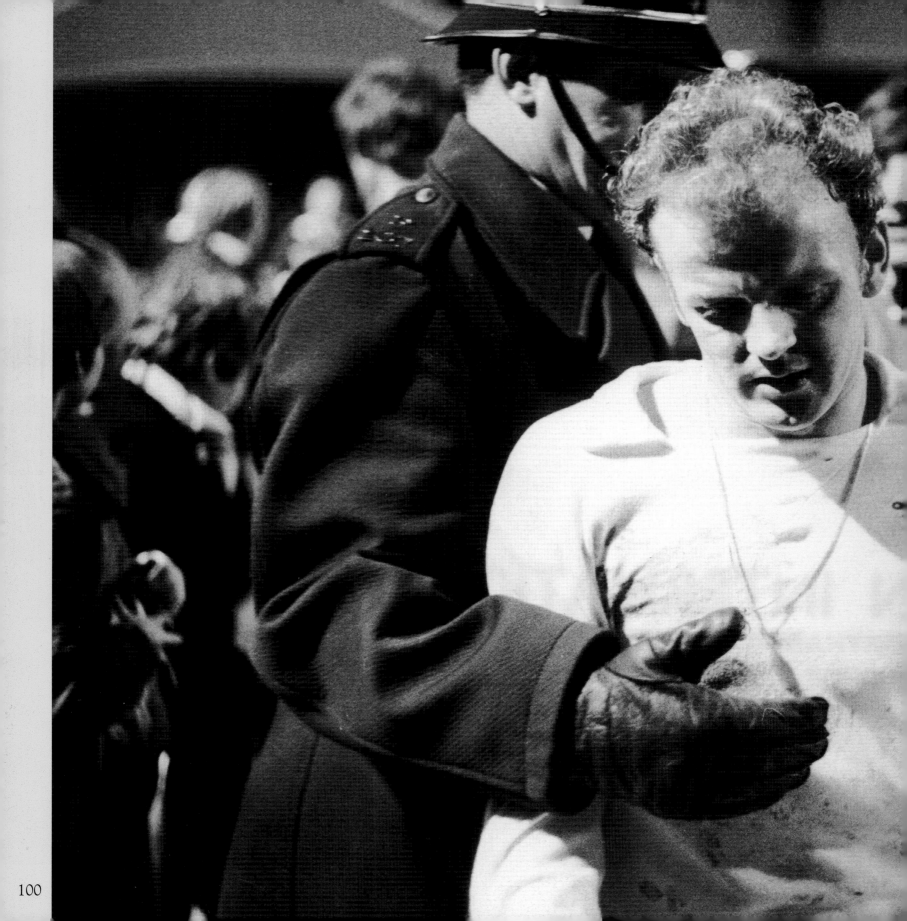

Mirror Sport

Tuesday, May 9, 1972
Telephone: (STD code 01)—353 0246

It's Derby's crown as Revie's men rage over lost penalties

NIGHT OF AGONY..

KEN JONES REPORTS Page 27

By PETER INGALL

LEEDS UNITED drove moodily away from Molineux last night, fuming over decisions by Swansea referee Bill Gow, which they felt robbed them of the championship. Wolves won 2—1.

Don Revie, the Leeds boss, said: "Naturally we are bitterly disappointed after all the hard work of the last nine months.

"But what can you do when the decisions go against you. We could have had three penalties. The first incident was definitely a penalty and if anyone has the picture on T.V. they will see that Bernard Shaw touched the ball with both hands.

"The second looked equally blatant when Phil Parkes brought down Allan Clarke and lay on top of him and I also thought there was another handling offence."

Derby got news of their Championship success last night after suffering anxious minutes in the lounge of their Majorca holiday hotel.

The team had interrupted their dinner to hear the dying minutes of the two vital games on the radio.

As the result from Wolves was known pandemonium broke out. Said assistant manager Peter Taylor: 'Everyone here seems to be Derby supporters. 'The glasses are being emptied, and two or three are parading shoulder high round the hotel.'

'Expectant'

Kevin Hector pushed through a wall of well wishers and commented: 'A few minutes ago we all had butterflies.

'Our courier said, 'I've just lost like a bunch of expectant fathers.' My God how right he was when we have given birth tonight to the League crown.'

Derby manager Brian Clough, speaking from the swish hotel in the Scilly Isles, claimed: 'I am the happiest man in the world.'

When he knew Derby had won the championship he ordered champagne all round for the fifty guests staying in the hotel.

Clough sent a message of congratulation to the Derby team and said he would see them next week for a private celebration.

UDT can lend you £800 for as little as £4 a week

— How would you like to borrow £800, with repayments as little as £4 a week? Or perhaps £1,000 for just £5 per week? This chance is yours now.

UDT KEY LOAN. With this new plan, you can borrow from £350 to several thousands, and with a really practical period of repayment, not 94 months. (This is calculated at today's interest rates, but your monthly repayment is guaranteed never to go up.)

Say you do decide to borrow £800. 'UDT Key Loan is a special scheme for home-owners, but UDT can also help you if you are not a house-owner. In fact, for the two schemes below, you don't even need a bank account.

UDT CREDIT LINE. Depending on your monthly payment, this plan enables you to draw up to £500. All at once, or in sums from £50. It's a really convenient way of budgeting for your needs—now, next month, next year, the year after.

UDT PERSONAL LOAN. Ideal for when you need a loan for a particular item—a colour TV, for example. You can borrow anything you need from £150 with up to 36 months for repayment.

A LOAN PLAN FOR EVERY NEED. As the rain's largest Finance House, UDT can help with any loan. And all UDT loan plans now qualify for tax relief. For further details, just fill in the coupon.

Please send me the booklet with details of your different loan plans. (Only available in Great Britain)

Name
Address

DMR 9/5

UDT United Dominions Trust (Commercial) Ltd. 51 Eastcheap, London EC3P 3BU. Tel: 01 623 3020.

HOW THEY FINISH

FIRST DIVISION

	P	W	L	D	F	A	Pts
DERBY	42	24	9	9	69	33	58
LEEDS	42	24	7	11	73	31	57
LIVERPOOL	42	24	9	9	64	30	57
MAN. CITY	42	23	11	8	77	45	57
ARSENAL	42	22	8	12	58	40	52
SPURS	42	19	13	10	63	42	51
CHELSEA	42	18	15	9	58	49	48
MAN. UTD.	42	19	10	13	69	61	48
WOLVES	42	18	11	13	65	57	47
SHEFF. UTD.	42	17	13	13	61	60	46

SUMMERBEE IN ALF'S SQUAD

By JACK STEGGLES

MANCHESTER CITY winger Mike Summerbee was yesterday called into the England squad for Saturday's Nations Cup quarter-final, second-leg clash with West Germany in Berlin.

The news was broken to Summerbee by City team manager Malcolm Allison and he went straight into Maine Road ground to collect his passport.

Summerbee's last appearance for England was against Switzerland at Wembley in November and he scored the goal in a 1—1 draw.

Allison confirmed yesterday that Francis Lee — who had earlier

pulled out of England's trip to Berlin—will also miss the home international championship.

In fact the Manchester City striker will not kiss another ball until August although he will be discharged from Bolton Royal Infirmary tomorrow — a day later than expected.

Said Allison: 'Francis is in need of a good rest and he will not be playing and any description until next season.'

Another blow for the Manchester City side last night was the news that Allan Clarke limped out

Norman Hunter, headed South to join up with England at their Hendon headquarters. Clarke travelled back to Leeds for treatment.

U.S. BLOCKADES VIETNAM

America to blockade all North Vietnamese ports, President Nixon announced. Mining already under way. Blockade would be lifted only when North Vietnamese released US prisoners and agreed to ceasefire.

© Daily Mirror Newspapers, Ltd, 1972

What a birthday! Jack Charlton, 37 yesterday, summed up the misery of the Leeds team whose League title hopes were destroyed by Wolves last night.

Printed and Published by DAILY MIRROR NEWSPAPERS, LTD. (01-353 0246) and for I.P.C Newspapers, Ltd. Holborn Circus, London, EC1P 1DQ. Registered at the Post Office as a newspaper.

K7

> "
> Forced to play 48 hours after the Cup final, Allan Clarke said:
>
> *We were the only team that won the FA Cup and never got to celebrate.*
> "

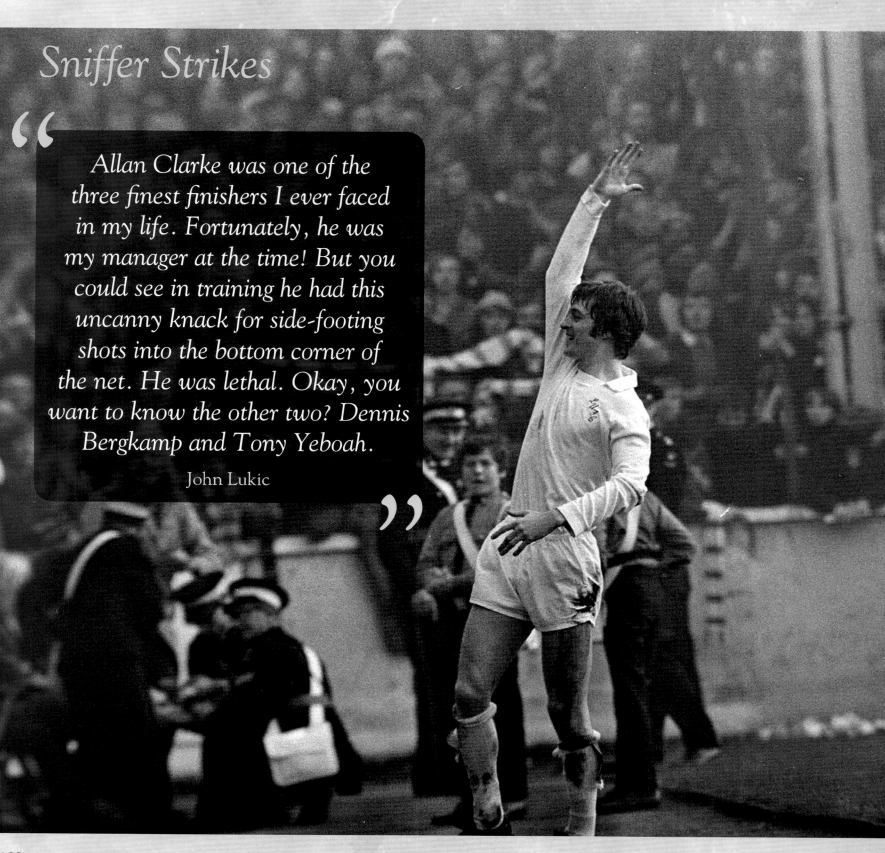

Sniffer Strikes

"

Allan Clarke was one of the three finest finishers I ever faced in my life. Fortunately, he was my manager at the time! But you could see in training he had this uncanny knack for side-footing shots into the bottom corner of the net. He was lethal. Okay, you want to know the other two? Dennis Bergkamp and Tony Yeboah.

John Lukic

"

Clarke as manager.

Turning On The Style

The sharpest kit, those distinctive number tags on their socks and personalized tracksuits – Leeds were football's fashion kings in the early Seventies and they gained an army of admirers as manager Don Revie took the shackles off his team and let them show their true virtuosity.

> *I admit we changed our style. In the first few years it was all about getting results. But for the last four or five years we were more attractive to watch, were at the top of every newspaper's popularity polls and won over many new fans. People loved watching us.*
>
> Don Revie

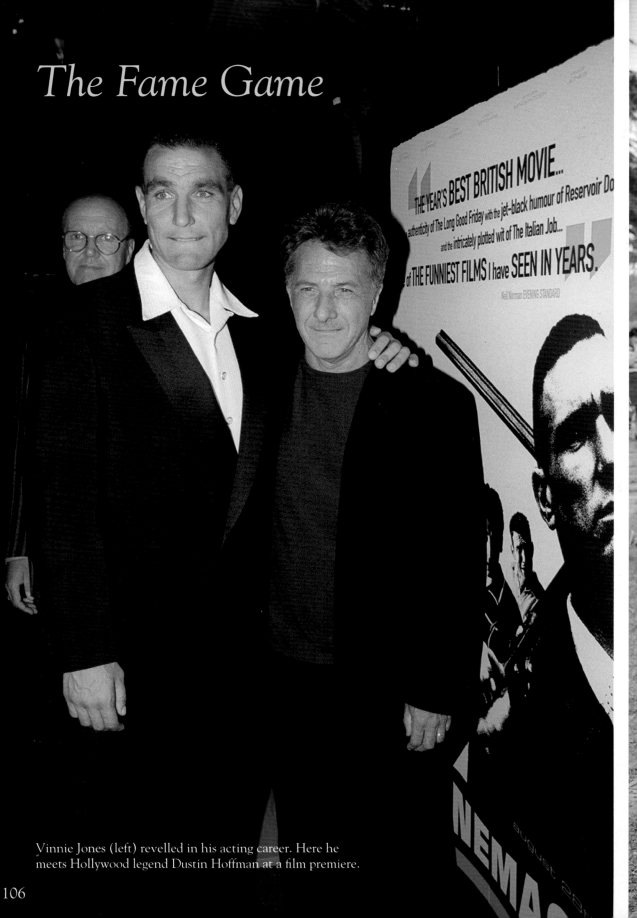

The Fame Game

Vinnie Jones (left) revelled in his acting career. Here he
meets Hollywood legend Dustin Hoffman at a film premiere.

The towering presence of three Leeds giants does not seem to intimidate their friends. In Lee Chapman's case he married actress Leslie Ash (above). And you have to salute Jack Charlton's good manners. On his visit to Pinewood Studios with the England World Cup squad in 1966 he at least found a step for actress Vivienne Ventura to stand on (above left). Mind, big Jack still towered over her.

The Cup
Of Cheer

The reigning FA Cup holders believed they were onto a good thing when they heard the Cup semi-final draw. They used to cross Elland Road and meet in a café for post-training tea.

The Cup Of Woe

Leeds and Sunderland were bitter adversaries again. Don Revie and Bob Stokoe were determined, opposing managers with little regard for each other. The top-flight side battered their Division Two opponents but failed to convert their superiority. Cue Ian Porterfield to score the only goal of the game, send Wearside mad and allow everybody else in football to have a sly grin at Leeds' misfortune. And Sunderland keeper Jim Montgomery also made himself a Wembley legend with a spectacular double save to deny Trevor Cherry and Peter Lorimer. It was a stunning disappointment for Revie and his team.

Revie consoles his players.

ABOVE: Revie and Stokoe lead out the teams.

RIGHT: Jim Montgomery's wonder save.

112

Shoot At 90 Mph?

The Elland Road Kop loved chanting "Ninety miles an hour" whenever Peter "Lash" Lorimer lined up a free-kick. His shooting power and accuracy were devastating. People often forget that he was the youngest player to make his Leeds debut at just 15 years and 289 days. He's also in the record books as the most prolific marksman in the club's history.

FOOTBALL
–STATS–
Peter Lorimer

Name: Peter (Patrick) Lorimer

Date of birth: 14th December 1946

Place of birth: Dundee, Scotland

Position: Right-winger, striker, midfield

Leeds career: 1963–79, 1984–85

Leeds appearances: 703

Leeds goals: 238

Scotland: 21 caps, 4 goals

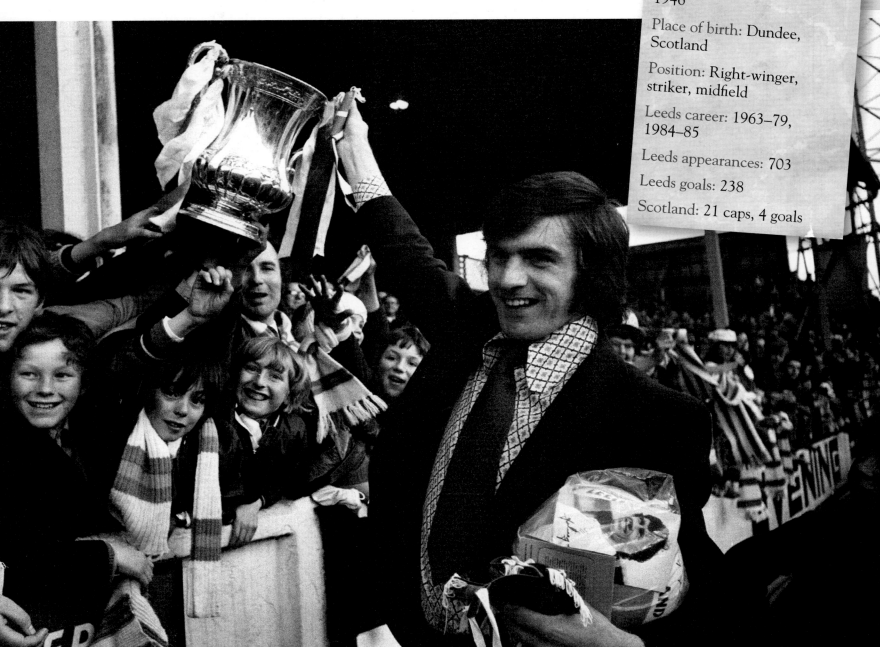

Cheated By Christos

Leeds faced AC Milan in the 1973 European Cup Winners' Cup final in Thessalonica. Leeds had goals disallowed and clear penalty claims dismissed by the Greek referee Christos Michas. Milan triumphed with a goal from an indirect free-kick, which was fired direct past David Harvey, as the winner. In the closing minutes Norman Hunter was sent off for retaliation after being cynically hacked as he pressed forward. The Leeds fans inside the stadium and the neutral Greeks in attendance made their feelings clear. Milan were jeered and whistled as they collected the trophy and their winners' medals. Michas was later convicted of match-fixing by a Greek court. He never refereed another game. He was fined, sent to jail and banned for life from refereeing.

The Leeds players are devastated.

Manager Revie consoles Mick Bates.

Hunter, sent to the dressing room, hopes the 10 men of Leeds might have grabbed a deserved equalizer.

A True Lap Of Honour

It reflects the madness of the occasion when the losers receive a standing ovation as the winners are jeered and booed off the park. But that's what happened when Leeds lost the 1973 European Cup Winners' Cup in controversial style in AC Milan.

Many years later a Euro MP tried to get the game and trophy officially handed to Leeds. UEFA, European football's governing body, had worked to drive out the match-fixers but changing the outcome of the final was a step too far.

ABOVE: Even in defeat Don Revie was proud of his players and consoles Peter Lorimer.

Tartan Army

BACK ROW: Joe Jordan, Dave Stewart, Gordon McQueen.
FRONT ROW: Eddie Gray, Peter Lorimer, Billy Bremner, Frank Gray.

There had always been a strong Scottish contingent at Elland Road, and this 1975 picture illustrates the point. As well as scouring Scotland for emerging talents like Eddie and Frank Gray and Billy Bremner, United also discovered great-value players by recruiting bargain signings from Scotland like Joe Jordan and Gordon McQueen.

"I'm no plastic Mac."

Tony Dorigo arrived at Leeds in a £1.3 million transfer from Chelsea and played a key role in the 1992 League title campaign. Although he was an Aussie, his British roots allowed Dorigo to choose between the home nations, and Gary Speed was clearly impressed by the kilt the full-back sported. But Dorigo opted to play for England and won 15 full caps.

119

Big Ed

In terms of versatility Paul Madeley was the greatest player seen in English football during the past 50 years. That is a strong claim but there isn't another player who could switch literally between any outfield position in a top-flight, honours-chasing team and make it look as if it was his chosen role. His intelligence, fitness and skills were quite astonishing. Madeley was so good that he could stand in for an injured international colleague and make the place his own. One week he could turn out at centre-forward – and score. The next game he'd trot out at left-back. Nothing fazed Madeley. Known as Big Ed, not Big 'Ead!, he was a very self-effacing, modest guy. Big Ed came from the name of a talking horse in a TV series of the Sixties. The Leeds players thought Paul spoke slowly and precisely, just like the talking horse.

Madeley, the stand-in striker sporting the number 9 shirt, scores against Manchester United.

FOOTBALL
–STATS–
Paul Madeley

Name: Paul Edward Madeley

Date of birth: 20th September 1944

Place of birth: Leeds

Position: Anywhere

Leeds career: 1963–80

Leeds appearances: 724

Leeds goals: 34

England: 24 caps, 0 goals

Entertaining footballers – or should that be keeping them out of mischief? – has always been a problem. There have been various attempts at achieving that goal at Leeds United down the years.

Snooker halls were frowned upon in the Fifties but that didn't stop Leeds having a snooker table inside the old West Stand. Intriguingly, the original caption of the picture taken in 1950 suggests the players are discussing football tactics with trainer Bob Roxburgh.

Don Revie perfected – and was later derided – for his team games of carpet bowls and bingo. Certainly Mick Bates, Jimmy Greenhoff and Rod Belfitt appear to be animated playing at table football in 1968.

Meeting the club chaplain.

123

Jack And The Beanstalk

Those who know Jack Charlton will confirm that, throughout his football career, one of his first questions on meeting an old mate was: "Have you got a ciggy?"

Big Jack and Billy Bremner were the star smokers in the Leeds camp. But this picture of Jack smoking was taken at the end of a photo shoot at the training ground next to Elland Road stadium.

In the background stands one of the pylons that were claimed to be the tallest in Europe when they were built in the early Seventies. They were about 240ft high and made Elland Road one of the easiest grounds to find – especially in the evening when they illuminated the south Leeds skyline. They were demolished when the new East Stand was built in 1993, with the floodlights being sited along the roof of the stand.

George Best?
Paul's Got Him In His Pocket!

> "
> *Paul was a terrific full-back. He was one of the quickest, fittest, hardest players I ever played with or against. You could tell right away he had that hunger. He would get everything out of the game that he wanted. And that he would deserve everything that he got. He was as straight as a die.*
>
> Johnny Giles
> "

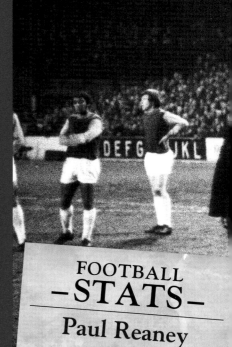

FOOTBALL
–STATS–
Paul Reaney

Name: Paul Reaney

Date of birth: 22nd October 1944

Place of birth: Fulham

Position: Right-back

Leeds career: 1962–78

Leeds appearances: 746

Leeds goals: 9

England: 3 caps, 0 goals

Paul Reaney was one of the great defenders of his generation. He didn't go out looking for plaudits because "Ra Ra", as he was nicknamed, was a true team player. In many respects he wasn't eye-catching. He was ruthlessly, at times devastatingly, efficient. Jack Charlton was discussing Reaney's strengths when he pointed out: "Make no mistake George Best was a truly great player. He could take defences apart but he rarely caused us problems when Manchester United played Leeds. Why? Because Don Revie would put Paul Reaney on George as a man marker. Paul was so good he could even put George in his pocket. He was that good."

Revie turns away as broken-leg victim Reaney is carried off at West Ham.

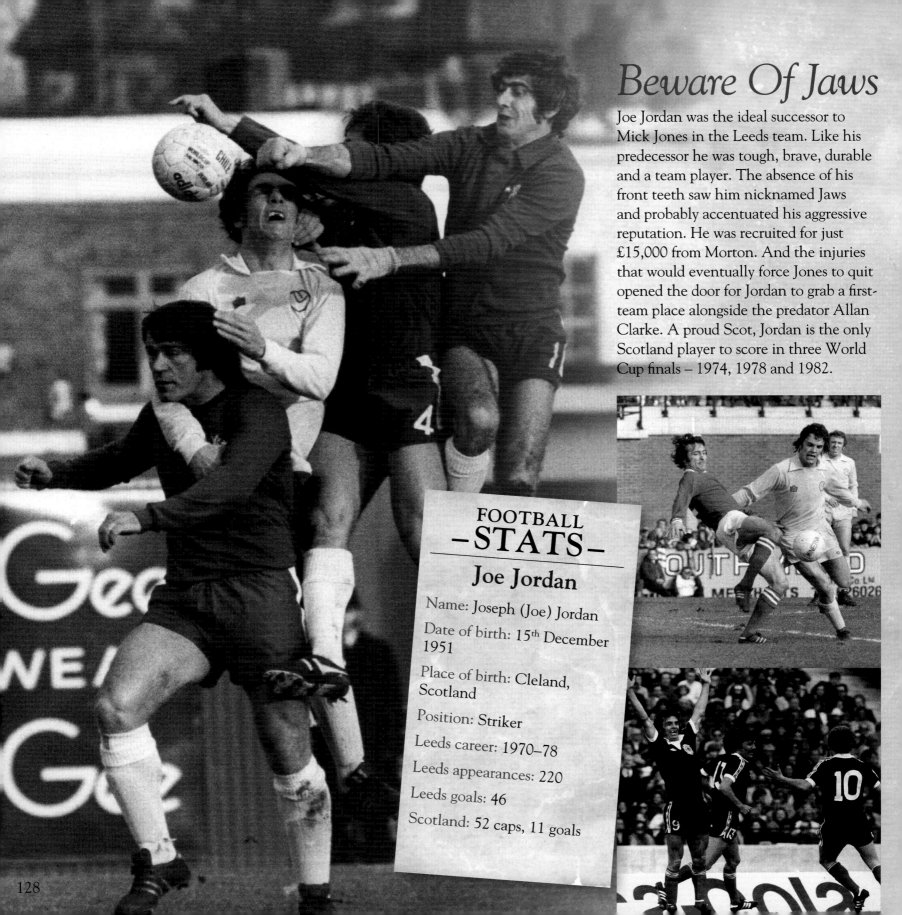

Beware Of Jaws

Joe Jordan was the ideal successor to Mick Jones in the Leeds team. Like his predecessor he was tough, brave, durable and a team player. The absence of his front teeth saw him nicknamed Jaws and probably accentuated his aggressive reputation. He was recruited for just £15,000 from Morton. And the injuries that would eventually force Jones to quit opened the door for Jordan to grab a first-team place alongside the predator Allan Clarke. A proud Scot, Jordan is the only Scotland player to score in three World Cup finals – 1974, 1978 and 1982.

FOOTBALL
–STATS–
Joe Jordan

Name: Joseph (Joe) Jordan

Date of birth: 15th December 1951

Place of birth: Cleland, Scotland

Position: Striker

Leeds career: 1970–78

Leeds appearances: 220

Leeds goals: 46

Scotland: 52 caps, 11 goals

'That's No Fairy, That's "Go Go"!

Gordon McQueen arrived at Leeds for a bargain £30,000 in 1972. He was seen by Don Revie as the towering defender who could eventually succeed veteran Jack Charlton.

It wasn't quite as simple as that for big "Go Go". In his early days the young McQueen was prone to make rash judgments, including attempts at racing forward in possession and often running into an opposition trap.

Initially, when big Jack was out, manager Don Revie preferred to deploy the supremely versatile Paul Madeley at centre-back but gradually McQueen won the manager over.

McQueen established himself alongside Norman Hunter in the 1973–74 title-winning team, which went 29 games before they lost a game.

Gordon was a larger-than-life character. He dressed as a fairy for Norman Hunter's testimonial performance of Cinderella. Billy Bremner was cast as Buttons.

Perhaps the biggest disappointment during McQueen's Leeds career was missing the European Cup final in 1975 through suspension. He had been sent off against Barcelona in the semi.

FOOTBALL —STATS—

Gordon McQueen

Name: Gordon McQueen

Date of birth: 26th June 1952

Place of birth: Kilbirnie, Scotland

Position: Centre-back

Leeds career: 1972–78

Leeds appearances: 171

Leeds goals: 19

Scotland: 30 caps, 5 goals

Bremner in action.

Bremner shoots against Manchester Utd.

If Don Revie had had his way Leeds would have had these two red-headed midfielders working in tandem. The Elland Road manager wanted to see Alan Ball playing his high-tempo, one-touch football alongside Billy Bremner and Johnny Giles. Unfortunately, Leeds couldn't meet Blackpool's asking price and Ball went to Everton.

133

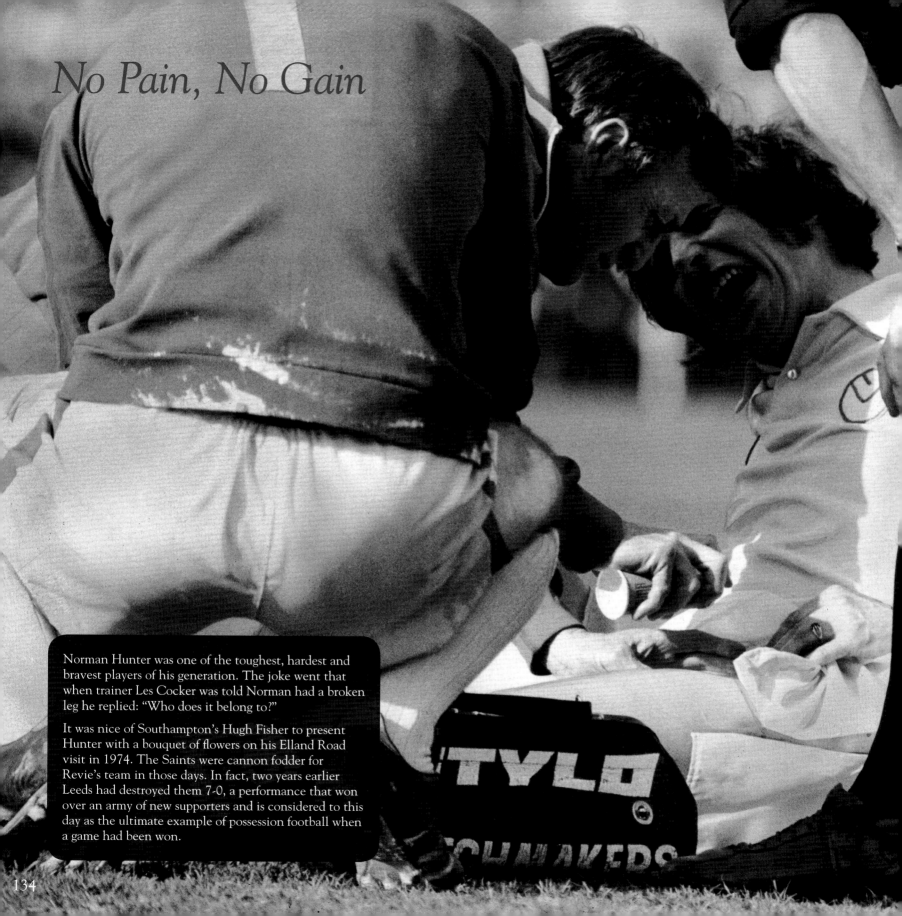

No Pain, No Gain

Norman Hunter was one of the toughest, hardest and bravest players of his generation. The joke went that when trainer Les Cocker was told Norman had a broken leg he replied: "Who does it belong to?"

It was nice of Southampton's Hugh Fisher to present Hunter with a bouquet of flowers on his Elland Road visit in 1974. The Saints were cannon fodder for Revie's team in those days. In fact, two years earlier Leeds had destroyed them 7-0, a performance that won over an army of new supporters and is considered to this day as the ultimate example of possession football when a game had been won.

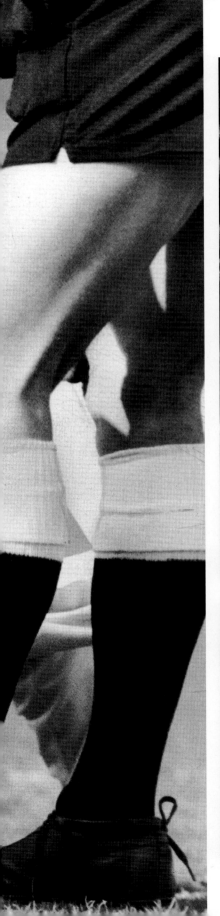

Hunter receiving flowers from Hugh Fisher.

Revie's Last Champs

Don Revie admitted after his departure that he didn't really want to leave Leeds.

    He had been the target for lucrative offers from other clubs at home and abroad for several years. He'd come close to leaving before. Now the England job was irresistible. But Don ensured that the squad he left behind was the best in England. He resigned after Leeds had been crowned champions again in 1974.

Bremner holds up the trophy.

The Three Lions Lure Revie

In the summer of 1974 Don Revie was the stand-alone candidate to succeed Sir Alf Ramsey as England manager. He was torn about leaving Elland Road but he finally decided to accept the FA offer and wear the Three Lions on his shirt.

REVIE'S HONOURS LIST WITH LEEDS

Between 1964 and 1974, Leeds won seven trophies but finished runners-up in a staggering 10 competitions.

1963–64 Second Division Champions
1964–65 Second in league, FA Cup finalists
1965–66 Second in league
1966–67 Fairs Cup finalists
1967–68 League Cup winners, Fairs Cup winners
1968–69 League Champions
1969–70 Second in league, FA Cup finalists
1970–71 Fairs Cup winners, second in league
1971–72 FA Cup winners, second in league
1972–73 FA Cup finalists, Cup Winners' Cup finalists
1973–74 League Champions

> *Don Revie was special. His ideas were well ahead of anybody else. He brought so many players through the youth system and knew how to get the best out of us. You cannot over-state what he did for Leeds United. Outside Yorkshire he isn't as revered as he should be. He took a struggling team and made us one of the best in Europe.*
>
> Norman Hunter

Revie leaves Elland Road on his last day.

Revie shakes hands with John Giles.

The Kingmaker

Don Revie weighed up the balance of power around Elland Road and nominated Johnny Giles as his successor. But it quickly became clear that chairman Manny Cussins and his board of directors were not listening to their departing boss.

> *Don is the most undervalued manager in history. Looking back, one of the sadnesses is that the board didn't take Don's advice and appoint Johnny Giles as his successor. If they had things might have been very different. Johnny was a clever man, a wonderful footballer. He would have had the confidence of everyone.*
>
> Lord Harewood, Leeds United president

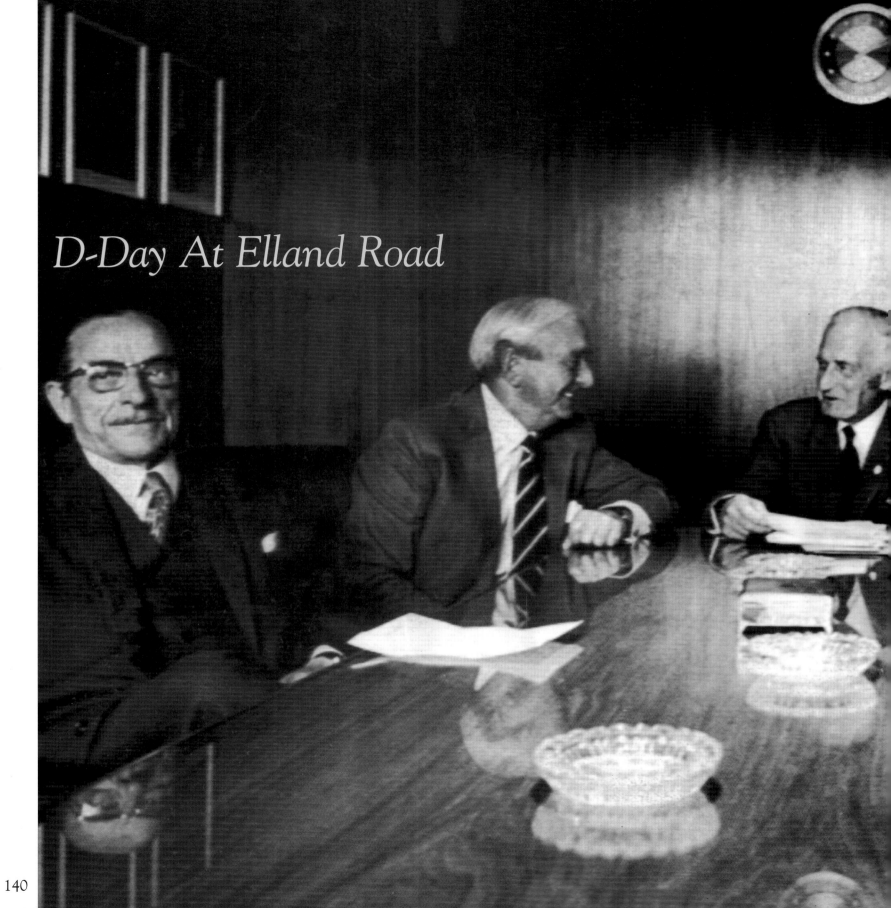

D-Day At Elland Road

This picture captures one of the most important, historic board meetings in the modern history of Leeds United. The directors were discussing who should succeed Don Revie as manager. Chairman Manny Cussins (centre) was making them aware that Revie had personally nominated an internal appointment – Johnny Giles.

They rejected Revie's proposal. During the same summer Liverpool were dealing with who should succeed the legendary Bill Shankly. They opted for an internal appointment in Bob Paisley, who proved to be even more successful at winning trophies than Shanks. Leeds decided to look outside Elland Road. The course of history changed dramatically.

> *Don told me he was recommending me as his successor. It was a possibility that had never, ever crossed my mind. A few days later Don phoned to say the board had rejected his recommendation. I believe whoever Don recommended would have been the last person the board wanted for the job.*
>
> Johnny Giles

If Only He Had Stuck By These
PRINCIPLES

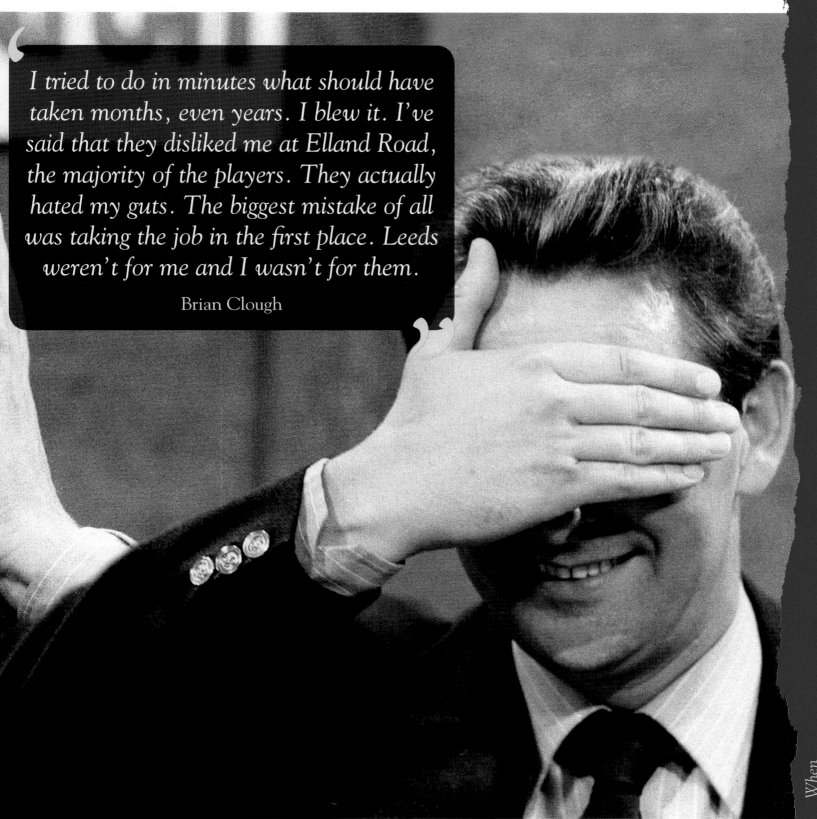

"I tried to do in minutes what should have taken months, even years. I blew it. I've said that they disliked me at Elland Road, the majority of the players. They actually hated my guts. The biggest mistake of all was taking the job in the first place. Leeds weren't for me and I wasn't for them."

Brian Clough

1970–71 Leeds win the Fairs Cup for the second time. A pitch invasion during a home defeat to West Brom sparks an FA investigation. Elland Road is closed and first four home games of the 71-72 season are played at neutral venues. 1971–72 Leeds reach the Centenary FA Cup final and beat Arsenal. Two days later they lose 2-1 at Wolves as they attempt to do the Double. 1972–73 Leeds finish third in the League but lose 1-0 to Sunderland in the FA Cup final. Leeds also lose to AC Milan in a controversial Cup-Winners' Cup final 1973–74 Leeds go 29 games before losing in the League, but after faltering still end up as champions. 1974–75 Don Revie leaves to take the England job. Brian Clough, his shock successor, only lasts 44 days before being sacked and replaced by Jimmy Armfield. Leeds finish ninth in the League but face Bayern Munich in the European Cup only to lose 2-0. 1975–76 Leeds finish fifth. 1976–77 Finish 10th in the League – their worst performance for 13 years. 1977–78 Crowd problems see the FA ban Leeds from playing FA Cup ties at Elland Road. Leeds finish ninth and sack Armfield. 1978–79 Jock Stein is recruited as manager. He never signs a contract and quits after 42 days to become Scotland manager. Jimmy Adamson succeeds Stein. Leeds finish fifth to qualify for the UEFA Cup. 1979–80 Attendances fall and Leeds finish 11th, scoring only 46 goals in 42 games. 1980–81 Adamson replaced by Allan Clarke after four defeats in opening five games. Leeds finish ninth. 1981–82 Leeds are relegated from the top flight. Clarke is sacked and replaced by Eddie Gray as player-manager. 1982–83 Facing financial crisis they finish eighth. 1983–84 Finish 10th. 1984–85 Finish seventh. 1985–86 After poor start and three months into the season Gray is sacked and is replaced by Billy Bremner. Leeds finish 14th. 1986–87 After finishing fourth in the League to reach the promotion play-offs. Leeds lose in extra-time to Charlton. 1987–88 Leeds finish seventh. 1988–89 Bremner is sacked after a poor start to the season. Leeds turn to Howard Wilkinson to rebuild the squad. 1989–90 Leeds win the Second Division title. 1990–91 John Lukic returns as Leeds' first £1million signing. Leeds fourth in the First Division. 1991–92 Manchester United put Leeds out of both domestic cup competitions but Leeds win the title. English champions for the third time. 1992–93 Leeds win Charity Shield beating Liverpool 4-3. Leeds slump to 17ᵗʰ in the first season of the Premier League, failing to win an away game. Glasgow Rangers win the Champions League Battle of Britain to put them out of Europe.

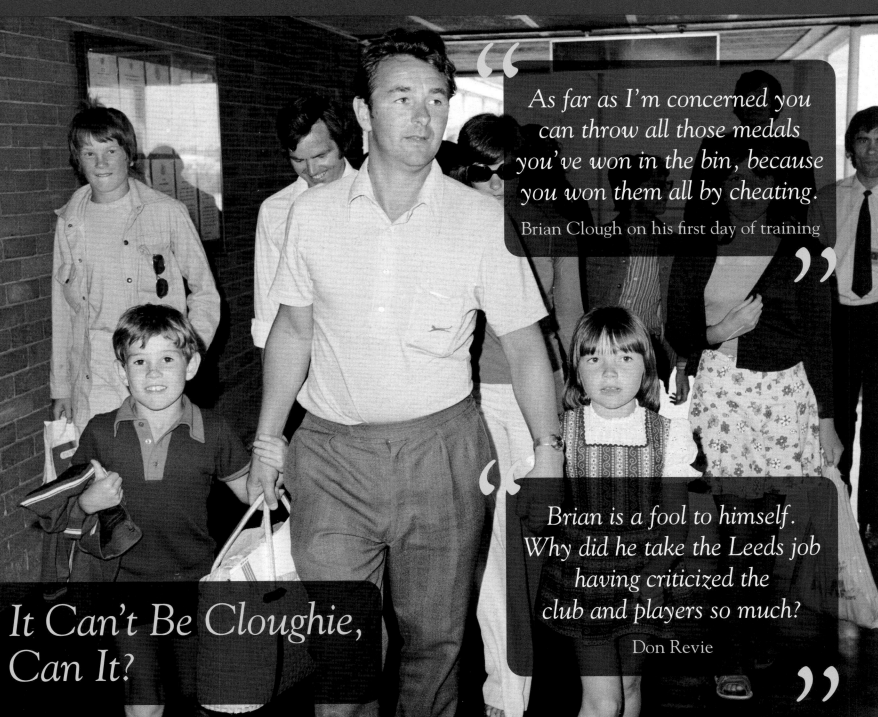

> " As far as I'm concerned you can throw all those medals you've won in the bin, because you won them all by cheating. "
>
> Brian Clough on his first day of training

> " Brian is a fool to himself. Why did he take the Leeds job having criticized the club and players so much? "
>
> Don Revie

It Can't Be Cloughie, Can It?

Yes THAT Photograph!

Brian Clough leads out Leeds United for the 1974 Charity Shield at Wembley, alongside Bill Shankly, who was making his farewell appearance as Liverpool boss, having retired a few weeks earlier. Clough later claimed he asked Don Revie to lead the champions out as his personal farewell and that Revie declined. A few days before the Wembley embarrassment Clough had been smiling in the Elland Road directors' box at a pre-season friendly. Ironically, the man on the row behind him is Allan Brown. He was Nottingham Forest manager at the time and the man Clough replaced at the City Ground in 1975.

Who Mentioned Charity?

It will go down in history as one of the most tawdry days in Charity Shield history – and it was meant to be so different.

Bill Shankly had retired as Liverpool manager that summer after winning the FA Cup but was invited by his successor Bob Paisley to lead out the Reds as a farewell gesture.

Brian Clough had been installed as the manager of champions Leeds. This was his first big game as United boss. But the game was besmirched by a series of ugly confrontations involving Liverpool's Kevin Keegan and Leeds' John Giles and Billy Bremner. It culminated in a flurry of punches and sending-offs for Bremner and Keegan.

If being sent off in a Wembley showpiece wasn't bad enough
Billy Bremner and Kevin Keegan compounded the felony.
    They caused outrage by tearing off their shirts and throwing
them to the ground on their way to the dressing rooms.

The Long Walk

Bremner heads to the tunnel.

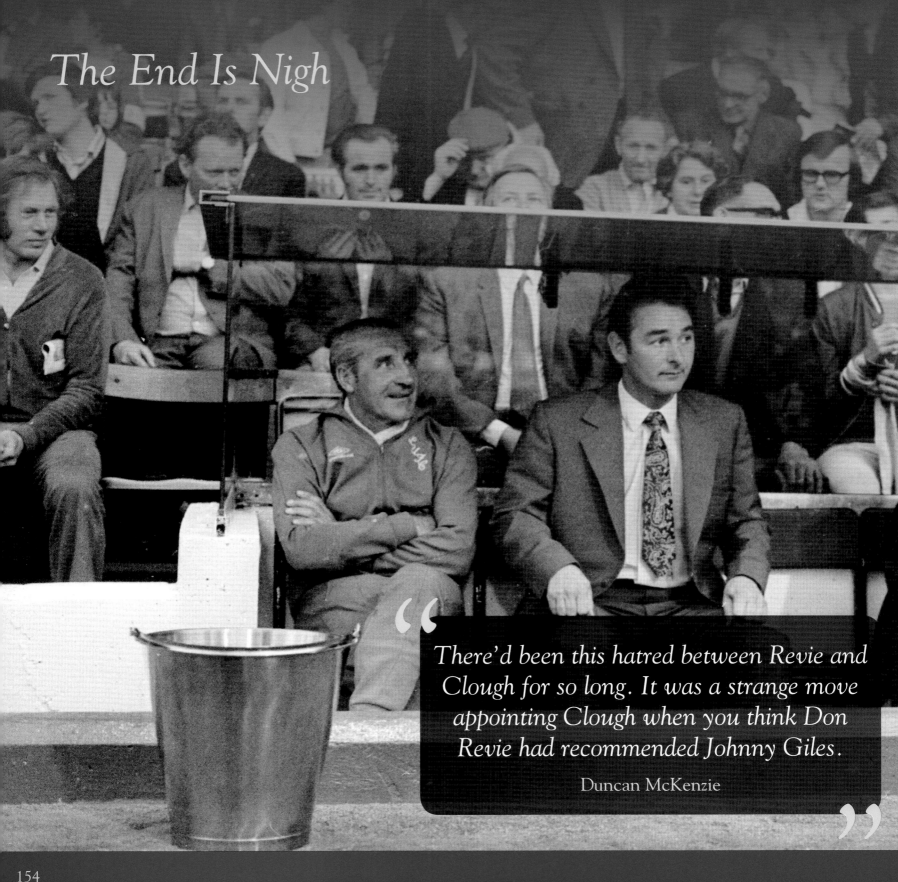

"There'd been this hatred between Revie and Clough for so long. It was a strange move appointing Clough when you think Don Revie had recommended Johnny Giles.

Duncan McKenzie"

> *He tried to change things too quickly. He thought he could get the broom out and everything Don Revie had achieved in the past 14 years would disappear. It wasn't going to be like that.*
>
> Eddie Gray

Mirror Sport

Saturday, September 14, 1974
Telephone: (STD code 01)—353 0246

CLOUGH SLAMS BILLY

By GRAHAM BAKER

'Bremner has to learn he is not boss of Leeds'

BRIAN CLOUGH, sacked after just forty-four days as manager of Leeds, talked last night about his bitter personality clash with skipper Billy Bremner.

FOSTER BOWS ONLY TO CLOCK!

By FRANK McGHEE

THE great Brendan Foster was beaten last night by the only opponent with any chance against him in his present world-beating form—THE CLOCK.

TOPS FOR WINNERS!

NAP!

NAP!

NAP!

4-PAGE RACING MIRROR PAGES 26–29

NEXT WEEK

YOUR CHANCE TO WATCH REVIE'S NEW ENGLAND

"After Years of BRONCHITIS I can walk for miles and run upstairs"

DO-DO

44 Days And Out

The football marriage that couldn't last ended after just 44 days. Most people insisted it was a crazy notion to recruit Brian Clough to manage players he had been so publicly critical of. Others, including a minority of Leeds players, say that if the board had stood by their beleagured boss Clough would have triumphed in the end.

" *This is a terrible day… for Leeds United.* "

Brian Clough

" *There is no doubt that Brian Clough failed at Leeds – or that he had proved before and would again later that he was a brilliant football manager.* "

Joe Jordan

Mirror Sport

Saturday, October 5, 1974
Telephone: (STD code 01)—353 0246

ARMFIELD IN HOT SEAT

He takes Revie's advice—and the big job at Leeds

Mario roars to super comeback

From MARK DOWONEY in New York

A FIERCE battle looms for tomorrow's United States Grand Prix.

By the end of the first practice sessions at Watkins Glen last night five drivers had smashed the previous qualifying lap record.

Mario Andretti led the field with a blistering time of 1m. 39.5s. It was a sensational comeback for the American driver who has been away from Grand Prix racing for nearly two years.

But Carlos Reutemann and his team-mate Carlos Pace in British - built Brabham Fords and Austria's Niki Lauda in a Ferrari put in times only fractionally slower.

Even the fifth man, South Africa's Jody Scheckter, was well inside the previous record set by Sweden's Ronnie Peterson last year.

The scorching pace of the early qualifying laps indicates that the struggle for the drivers world championship will be the toughest ever.

Co-favourites for Jackie Stewart's vacated crown, Clay Regazzoni and Emerson Fittipaldi, could make no impression on yesterday's fast times.

They will be forced to pull something out of the bag in today's final practice if they are to get a good starting position.

Dan's big fight is knocked out —by the flu

By JACK STEGGLES

THE British heavyweight title fight between Dan McAlinden and Bunny Johnson—scheduled for Wolverhampton next Tuesday—has been called off because McAlinden has 'flu.

The Champion McAlinden, who has not defended his title since he took it from Jack Bodell in June 1972, was unable to get out of bed yesterday. A doctor confirmed that he would not be fit to fight for at least a month.

JIMMY ARMFIELD took over the Leeds United hot-seat yesterday—after talks with former Elland Road boss Don Revie.

He discussed his future with England's new manager in midweek and, I understand, the possibility of a top job outside club management.

Armfield, 39, was himself on the short-list for the England job after the sacking of Sir Alf Ramsey last season.

By KEVIN MOSELEY

Bolton manager and former England full back, Armfield was offered a £64,000 four-year contract by Leeds a week ago.

And Revie's advice obviously played a part in Armfield's decision to take over at Leeds, where Brian Clough lasted only 43 days.

Armfield said: "I had virtually decided last night that I would take the job, but I said all along that I would give a decision on Friday.

"After turning down jobs at Everton and Sheffield United, I decided that I now have enough experience for a job of this magnitude. And I have now got to find out what I'm capable of.

"It is my job to stabilise things at Leeds. The assets of the club must make it one of the highest ranking in the land and I am delighted to get the chance to go there.

"There comes a time when you have to make decisions. This is a great challenge for me."

Leeds, last season's champions, have slumped to fourth from the bottom in their weeks of upheaval.

Confident

Armfield is confident that he will be able to put together the shattered pieces.

"If I fall on my face, then that's it," said Armfield. "You don't know what you're capable of doing until you try.

"If my 13-year-old son Duncan had been, say, 18 months older, I would not have taken the job.

"My move had to be made now or not at all. I am a firm believer

in a child's education. If the lad had been coming up for his 'O' levels, it would not have moved.

"I couldn't uproot the family at this stage in a child's life. I could have stayed on at Bolton if they were prepared to keep me."

Armfield dismissed any suggestion that he had been worried about the player-power which was considered one reason for Clough's exit.

Watcher

He will watch today's home match with Arsenal but will not take control until Monday.

Assistant manager Ian Greaves will be in charge at Bolton until the board decide whether to look elsewhere for Armfield's successor.

Arsenal recall? George Armstrong against Leeds in place of Charlie George, who cracked a toe bone at Arsenal's match on Wednesday.

Rangers bring in Mancini

TERRY MANCINI involved in a bitter row with Queen's Park Rangers last week, makes a dramatic return against First Division leaders Ipswich today, writes Jack Steggles.

Transfer-listed Mancini thirty-one yesterday comes back in place of David Webb who missed training to go to hospital for X-rays on a damaged ankle.

But the surprise recall has not changed Mancini's determination to get away from the club who a month ago told him he was no longer wanted.

He was put on the list at £15,000—but Arsenal were asked for £30,000 when they made a shock move for him. Arsenal promptly ended their interest.

Decided

Mancini told me last night: "It's great to be back and I shall be doing everything I can to help Rangers.

"But nothing has changed. Rangers decided they had no further use for me. They put me on the list and I'm still on it."

Rangers, who have Stan Bowles back after a two-match ban, are opposed by former manager Gordon Jago, had good news yesterday about Frank McLintock.

McLintock — yet to appear in the first team this season because of a heel injury — played in the third team today and expects to be ready for a first team call in midweek.

ZIP GOES A MILLION

Manchester City had an income of more than £1 million for the first time in their history last season, but they still showed a loss of £160,400.

United have Jim Holton back at centre half after suspension and £200,000 striker Stuart Pearson has recovered from injury.

Fulham expect to bank record takings from the visit of the Second Division leaders.

All 9,000 seats have been sold and Fulham anticipate a crowd of around 25,000—which will bring in £15,000 receipts.

Off to Leeds . . . Jimmy Armfield leaves Bolton with a handful of boots and his track suit inside a newspaper.

LLOYD SHOCK FOR FULHAM

FULHAM received a shock yesterday when midfield man Barry Lloyd limped into the ground with a bruised and swollen left ankle.

Lloyd had treatment all day yesterday and will receive more this morning in a bid to be fit to face Manchester United.

Lloyd said: "I got a knock on the ankle when we played Norwich

with a couple of weeks ago.

"It has not caused me too much bother. But when I woke this morning it was very painful and I can only put it down to the fact that it was jarred on Wednesday when I played squash.

"It is a lot easier now and I really hope to be fit—for this is one game I want to be involved in."

Printed and Published by THE DAILY MIRROR NEWSPAPERS, Ltd. (01-353 0246) at, and for IPC Newspapers Ltd., Holborn Circus, London, EC1P 1DQ. Registered at the Post Office as a newspaper. © The Daily Mirror Newspapers, Ltd., 1974.

The Leeds board again cast around for a new manager. Chairman Manny Cussins called Johnny Giles to an early morning meeting, suggesting he would be offered the job. When the Irishman arrived at Elland Road he discovered the board also wanted to interview Billy Bremner for the vacancy. The split board voted 3–2 for Giles. Giles told them he was not interested in the job if they weren't all backing him. Enter Jimmy Armfield from Bolton Wanderers. And who had genial Jim consulted before taking the job? Of course, Don Revie.

Eddie Gray was a breathtakingly skilful player and was blessed with that precious gift of being able to dribble past opponents. While other players passed sublimely and others had pace to burn, Eddie had genuine stamina and the ability to paint the most intricate patterns with his skills and wing sorcery.

Elland Road was a muddy mess on the day Leeds played Burnley but Gray despatched the kind of goal, involving drag-backs and shimmies, that Lionel Messi or Diego Maradona would be proud to claim as their own.

Sadly, injuries cut Eddie down in his prime. He remained popular in the dressing room as he battled bravely to overcome a thigh muscle condition that might have finished lesser men. That's why Brian Clough's ill-judged remark that Gray would have been shot if he had been a racehorse went down so badly with the Leeds players. Ironically, after all that time on the treatment table, Gray was still turning out as Leeds' player-manager in his 35th year.

> " Brian said if I'd been a horse he would have shot me. He might have been right. I'd had a lot of injuries. But he could have said that a bit better, too. I don't think that endeared him to the players especially coming from someone who'd had to pack in the game through injury. He might have forgotten that happened to him. "
>
> Eddie Gray

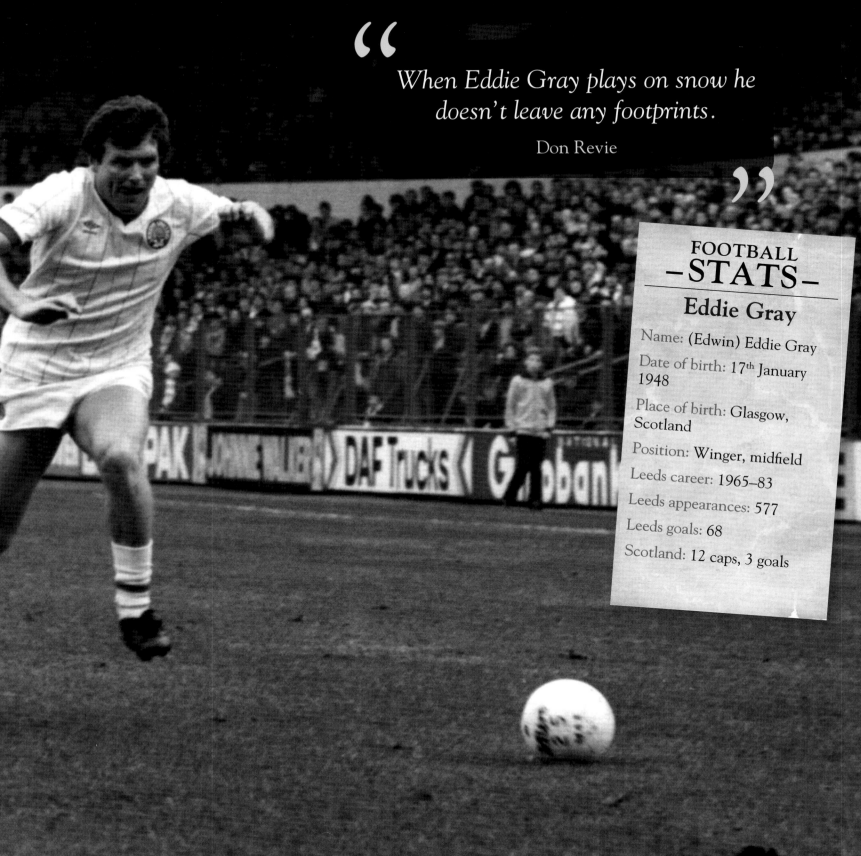

> "When Eddie Gray plays on snow he doesn't leave any footprints."
>
> Don Revie

FOOTBALL
–STATS–

Eddie Gray

Name: (Edwin) Eddie Gray

Date of birth: 17th January 1948

Place of birth: Glasgow, Scotland

Position: Winger, midfield

Leeds career: 1965–83

Leeds appearances: 577

Leeds goals: 68

Scotland: 12 caps, 3 goals

The Changing
Face Of Leeds

RIGHT: Terry Yorath, a homegrown player discovered in south Wales, became the heir apparent to Giles and Bremner in the Leeds midfield.

BELOW: Celebrations at Chelsea.

162

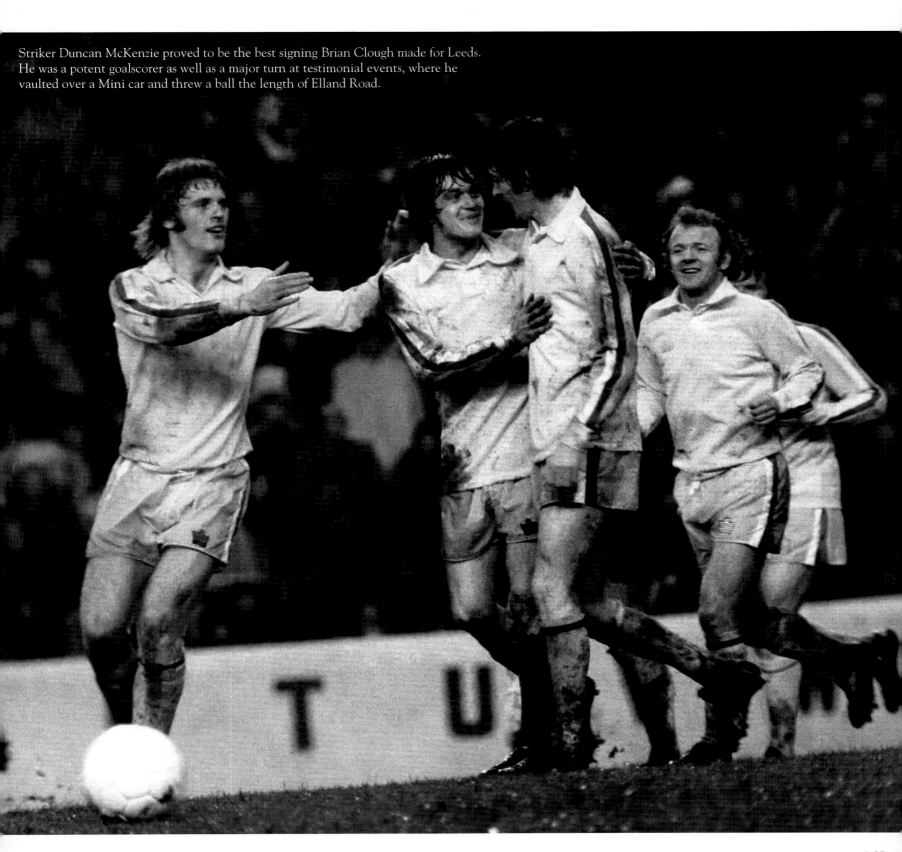

Striker Duncan McKenzie proved to be the best signing Brian Clough made for Leeds. He was a potent goalscorer as well as a major turn at testimonial events, where he vaulted over a Mini car and threw a ball the length of Elland Road.

The Final
Euro Insult

Jimmy Armfield steadied the sinking ship and guided
Leeds into the European Cup final against Bayern Munich
in Paris. But the horrific memories of old with appalling
decisions going against them haunted the English
champions. Nobody could dispute that Franz Beckenbauer
tripped Allan Clarke to concede a penalty. Everybody in
the Parc des Princes saw it apart from the man who had to
award the spot-kick.

Frankly He's Great

Frank Gray may have been the biggest beneficiary of Brian Clough's crazy reign at Elland Road. The younger brother of Eddie was supposed to be one of the bright young players who would take on the challenge of maintaining the club's success in the post-Revie era. Sadly, it wasn't to be. Frank played in the 1975 European Cup final defeat against Bayern Munich but in 1979 was sold to Nottingham Forest for £500,000. This time he enjoyed success with Clough. Frank was in the 1980 Forest side that beat Hamburg SV to win the European Cup. Gray was the first British player to appear for different clubs in two European Cup finals. He did return to Elland Road for a second stint. He was brought back by Allan Clarke but the decline and fall of Leeds out of the top flight was imminent.

FOOTBALL –STATS–
Frank Gray

Name: (Francis) Frank (Tierney) Gray

Date of birth: 27th October 1954

Place of birth: Glasgow, Scotland

Position: Left-back

Leeds career: 1972–79, 1981–85

Leeds appearances: 405

Leeds goals: 35

Scotland: 32 caps, 1 goal

Frank Gray holds off Middlesbrough midfielder Graeme Souness.

Frank Gray (front row left) with the Nottingham Forest team that won the 1980 European Cup final.

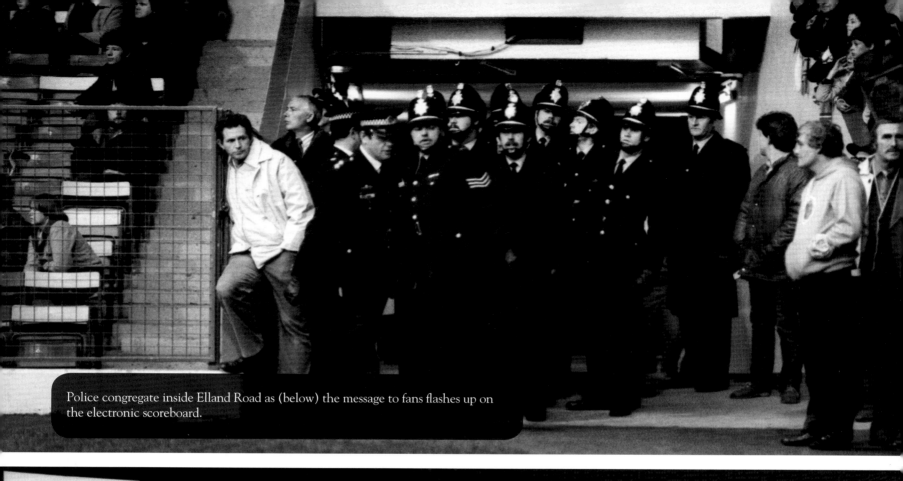

Police congregate inside Elland Road as (below) the message to fans flashes up on the electronic scoreboard.

LEEDS & UNITED
NEW DOUBLE GAME
LOTTERY TICKETS 25p

LEEDS UTD.   NEWCASTLE

0   0

Radio
Aire
FIRST FOR SPORT

PLEASE
BEHAVE

Crowd Troubles

The decline and fall of Leeds sadly sparked increasingly frequent crowd disorder.

From the Seventies through to the Eighties there was a major issue with Leeds fans and violent behaviour. It was a problem that had to be resolved and it even crept up on the club in 1990 when promotion back to the top flight was marred by violence outside Bournemouth's Dean Court ground.

Leeds travel for a Cup-tie to Wigan and the mounted police wait for an emergency call to quell crowd disorder.

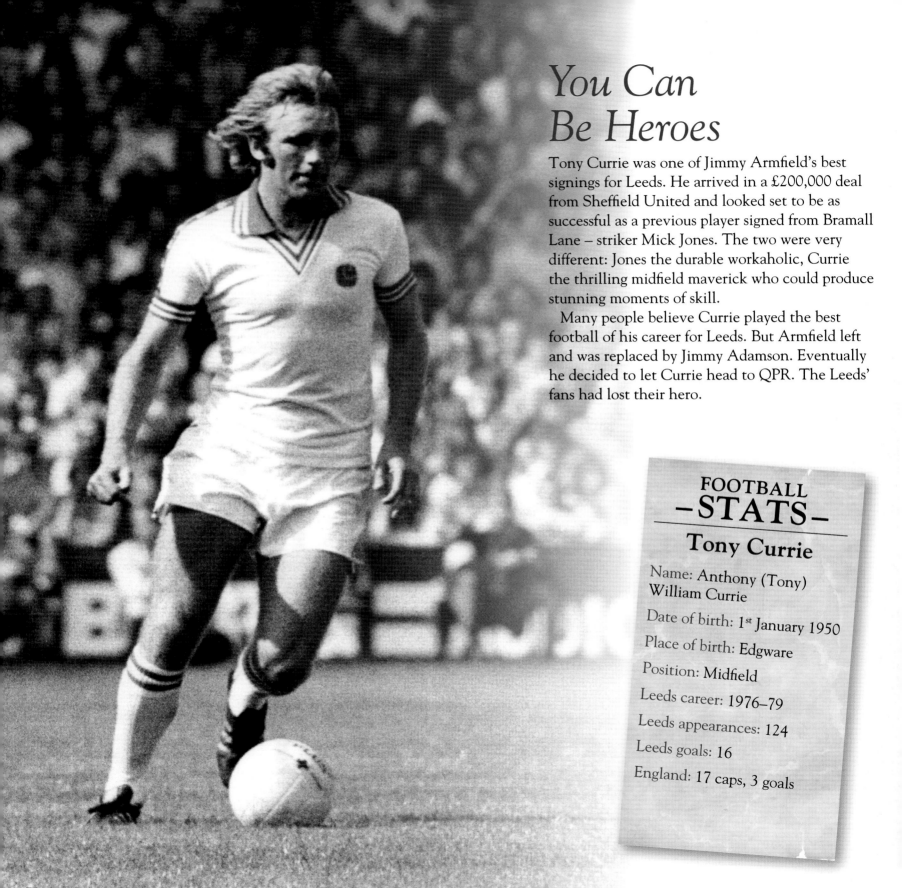

You Can Be Heroes

Tony Currie was one of Jimmy Armfield's best signings for Leeds. He arrived in a £200,000 deal from Sheffield United and looked set to be as successful as a previous player signed from Bramall Lane – striker Mick Jones. The two were very different: Jones the durable workaholic, Currie the thrilling midfield maverick who could produce stunning moments of skill.

Many people believe Currie played the best football of his career for Leeds. But Armfield left and was replaced by Jimmy Adamson. Eventually he decided to let Currie head to QPR. The Leeds' fans had lost their hero.

FOOTBALL -STATS-
Tony Currie

Name: Anthony (Tony) William Currie

Date of birth: 1st January 1950

Place of birth: Edgware

Position: Midfield

Leeds career: 1976–79

Leeds appearances: 124

Leeds goals: 16

England: 17 caps, 3 goals

Alex Sabella about to receive a tackle.

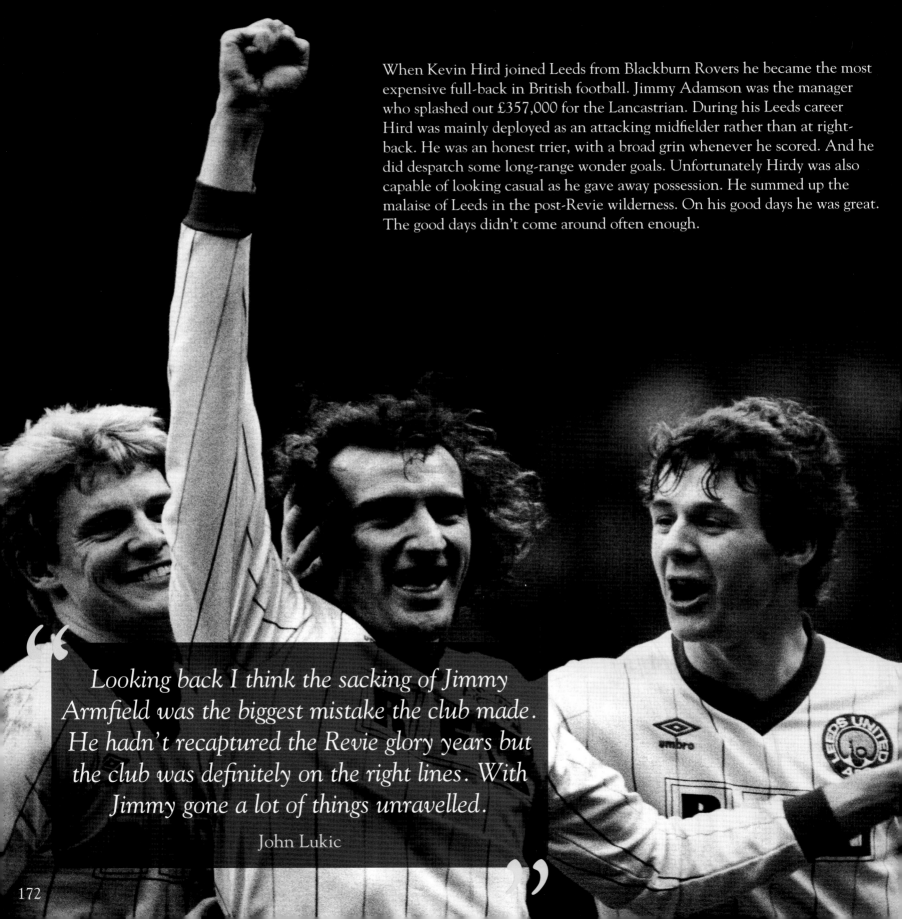

When Kevin Hird joined Leeds from Blackburn Rovers he became the most expensive full-back in British football. Jimmy Adamson was the manager who splashed out £357,000 for the Lancastrian. During his Leeds career Hird was mainly deployed as an attacking midfielder rather than at right-back. He was an honest trier, with a broad grin whenever he scored. And he did despatch some long-range wonder goals. Unfortunately Hirdy was also capable of looking casual as he gave away possession. He summed up the malaise of Leeds in the post-Revie wilderness. On his good days he was great. The good days didn't come around often enough.

"

Looking back I think the sacking of Jimmy Armfield was the biggest mistake the club made. He hadn't recaptured the Revie glory years but the club was definitely on the right lines. With Jimmy gone a lot of things unravelled.

John Lukic

"

Frank Worthington bravely heads home Leeds' first goal in their 3-1 win over Newcastle in October 1982.

That Sinking Feeling

Nobody could dispute the job Trevor Cherry and Paul Hart did in trying to keep Leeds afloat in the top flight. Cherry stayed at Elland Road as one of the final links with the Revie days. Hart, signed by Jimmy Armfield as Gordon McQueen's replacement, had overcome a nightmare start beset by own goals to prove himself a tough, resilient defender.

But Leeds' financial plight worsened after relegation in 1982. Hart was sold to Brian Clough's Nottingham Forest the following year for just £40,000. While Leeds floundered he spent the next four seasons in the top flight with Forest and Sheffield Wednesday.

FOOTBALL
–STATS–
Trevor Cherry

Name: Trevor John Cherry

Date of birth: 23rd February 1948

Place of birth: Huddersfield

Position: Defender

Leeds career: 1972–82

Leeds appearances: 481

Leeds goals: 31

England: 27 caps, 0 goals

Paul Hart in action.

They Tried And Failed

Some fine players tried and failed to rekindle the good times at Elland Road. Kenny Burns (right) had been voted Footballer of the Year during his days at Nottingham Forest. He was even handed the captaincy at Leeds in an attempt to add some Glaswegian toughness to the team. It didn't work.

Brian Greenhoff (opposite) arrived from Manchester United but injuries and weight issues saw the former England star's career go into decline.

Eight years after Don Revie left Leeds to become England manager it was Allan Clarke (left) who was in charge when Leeds were relegated. Clarke spent a club record £930,000 on winger Peter Barnes, who flopped badly. Leeds struggled for goals and were dispatched to Division Two. Relegation cost Clarke his job.

He joined the list – which included Jimmy Armfield, Jock Stein (above) and Jimmy Adamson – of those who found Don's shoes impossible to fill.

179

There's Only One Shez

John Sheridan played with a style and a swagger that made him a Leeds hero even though the club was toiling to escape Division Two. His calling card was the expertise he could produce, with regard to free-kicks in particular; when a free-kick was rolled to him, he'd flick the ball into the air before dispatching an unstoppable volley over the opposition's defensive wall.

FOOTBALL –STATS–

John Sheridan

Name: John Joseph Sheridan

Date of birth: 1st October 1964

Place of birth: Stretford

Position: Midfield

Leeds career: 1982–89

Leeds appearances: 264

Leeds goals: 52

Republic of Ireland: 34 caps, 5 goals

John Sheridan (left) and skipper Brendan Ormsby celebrate United's 3-2 win over Ipswich in October 1987.

Battling Baird

In the dark days of Division Two Ian Baird offered those priceless qualities of commitment, aggression and determination. He wasn't the best striker seen at Elland Road down the years but the crowd warmed to his whole-hearted style of play even if, at times, his aggressive streak led him into predictable disciplinary problems. Bairdy was hard-working and hard. He remained popular at Elland Road when he returned, but the fact was that under Howard Wilkinson a plan was developing to take the club to new heights.

FOOTBALL
–STATS–

Iain Baird

Name: Ian Baird

Date of birth: 1st April 1964

Place of birth: Rotherham

Position: Striker

Leeds career: 1985–87, 1988–90

Leeds appearances: 192

Leeds goals: 58

Whatever Happened To The Birthday Boy?

It's February 1990 and young Simon Grayson (centre) is celebrating his 21st birthday with some famous colleagues. There are, of course, two Leeds managers of the future in the picture. As well as Grayson there's Gary McAllister (front right) who was in charge at Leeds in 2008.

25 years earlier in the players' lounge.

185

Wilko

Few managers have ever had the kind of positive impact on a new club that Howard Wilkinson inspired at Leeds. After three Revie old boys had tried and failed to spark an Elland Road revival the board persuaded Wilko to step down from Division One Sheffield Wednesday to mastermind United's renaissance.

Wilkinson initially met chairman Leslie Silver and convinced him there was a high-speed route for Leeds to storm back into the big time but that he would require financial commitment from the top. Silver made that pledge and an exciting raft of players brought in by Wilkinson duly transformed United's fortunes. From the lower reaches of the old Division Two Leeds were transformed by the likes of Gordon Strachan, Chris Fairclough, Chris Kamara and Vinnie Jones.

> " It may surprise people that at my interview I actually outlined a ten year plan for Leeds. On the face of it moving to Leeds was crazy. I was manager of a club that was seventh in the First Division and I was joining a club four places above relegation to Division Three. "
>
> Howard Wilkinson

The Arrival Of King Tongue

Gordon Strachan was always a quick-witted epitome of the small man who won't let anyone kick sand in his face.

But few people remember that when he first arrived at Elland Road he was low on confidence. He'd endured a rocky spell at Manchester United where he had not enjoyed being reunited with his former Aberdeen manager Alex Ferguson.

The move across the Pennines was great for Leeds United. It was also a massive tonic for Strachan who relished the responsibility thrust on his shoulders as the team's skipper, elder statesman and on-field inspiration.

Strachan with Alex Ferguson.

> *For a man so small in size he's a person of great stature who can destroy the tough guys in the dressing room with one lash of his coruscating tongue. That's why at Leeds he earned the nickname 'King Tongue'.*
>
> Howard Wilkinson

Strachan with Scotland team-mate Kenny Dalglish.

The Ginger-Headed Inspiration

Strachan holds aloft the
Championship trophy in 1992.

Scotland team-mates Graeme Souness (left), Alan Hansen, Kenny Dalglish, Willie Miller and Gordon Strachan in 1980.

Skipper Gordon Strachan ensures Gary Speed is fit and ready to return for action as Leeds close in on the 1992 title. Strachan had recognized the full value of the young Welshman's efforts in midfield. Speed was part of a midfield quartet – with Strachan, David Batty and Gary McAllister – which provided the bedrock of United's championship campaign. They provided the perfect compliment of skill and strength.

"

In many respects I believe Gary Speed was the most outstanding player in our title-winning season. He switched to full-back and striker in times of emergency. He was a totally reliable member of our squad.

Howard Wilkinson

"

Rod Wallace

> " *After joining us with his brother Ray from Southampton Rod made a slow start. One or two people began to doubt him but once he found his scoring touch there was no stopping him and we kept seeing that lovely, broad grin as he celebrated his goals.*
>
> Howard Wilkinson
> "

Lee Chapman

If Howard Wilkinson had been able to persuade Wolves to sell Steve Bull, the sight of Lee
Chapman in a Leeds shirt may never have come about. But Wolves were adamant their goal
machine could not be prised out of Molineux so the Leeds boss went in search of another proven
goalscorer, and a man he knew very well. Chapman was prised out of Nottingham Forest and
reunited with the manager he'd worked with at Sheffield Wednesday.

The duo had enjoyed success at Hillsborough. At Elland Road Chappy enjoyed the time of his
life. He was a crucial part of the team that won the Division Two title, finished fourth and then
won the Division One title.

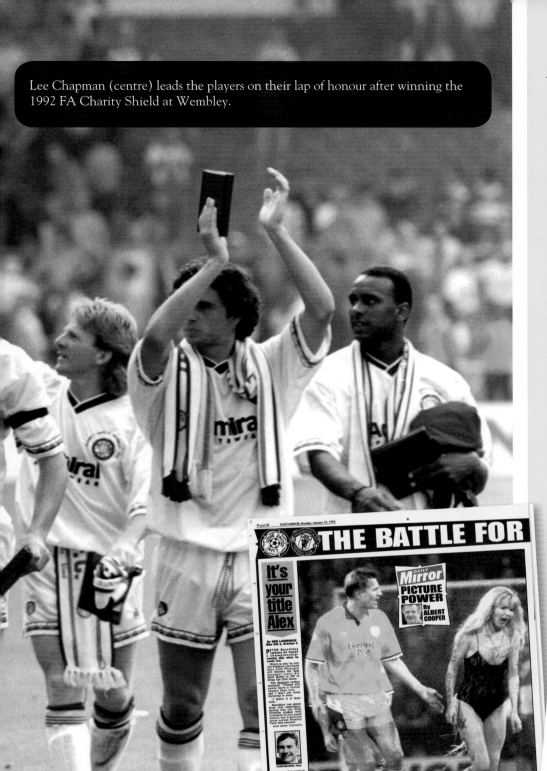

Lee Chapman (centre) leads the players on their lap of honour after winning the 1992 FA Charity Shield at Wembley.

LEE CHAPMAN'S Clubs:

1978–82 Stoke City
1978 Plymouth (on loan)
1982–83 Arsenal
1983–84 Sunderland
1984–88 Sheffield Wednesday
1988 Niortais
1988–90 Nottingham Forest
1990–93 Leeds United
1993 Portsmouth
1993–95 West Ham
1995 Southend (on loan)
1995–96 Ipswich Town
1996 Leeds United (on loan)
1996 Swansea City
1996 Strømsgodset IF

197

When Leeds were toiling and needed someone to come up with a barnstorming run to change the mood of the game and inspire people, they depended on two heroes. Skipper Gordon Strachan was the obvious man. The other was attacking right-back Mel Sterland. The Sheffield-born defender would gallop forward, break through tackles and deliver the pinpoint crosses that Lee Chapman relished.

WE ARE THE

Child's play for Howard

By JOHN EDWARDS and HARRY HARRIS

HOWARD WILKINSON completed a meteoric rise to soccer's summit last night and admitted: "I'm overcome by it all."

Wilko was confirmed as Leeds' first title-winning boss in 18 years – but he had to be told about it by his five-year-old son Ben!

For while the rest of the nation tuned into United's agonising near-miss on TV, the 48-year-old Tyke calmly tucked into roast beef and Yorkshire pud with friends and relatives at his Sheffield home.

Little Ben couldn't bear the tension and sneaked upstairs to watch the drama unfold on a spare set. And when he shouted down that first Ian Rush then substitute Mark Walters had put the title beyond United's reach, the news was greeted with shrieks of delight.

Wilkinson explained his amazingly low-key approach to the biggest moment of his career by saying: "All I was interested in once the Sheffield United match was over was getting home for my Sunday lunch.

"Never mind getting all the players together at Elland Road to watch the Anfield match on TV or even watching it in my own home.

"The plan was always just to get back and have a bit of a lunch party with a few friends.

"I must admit I feel overcome. This is the most fantastic day of my life. It's the classic dream-come-true."

But overjoyed Wilko could still spare a thought for Fergie, saying: "I know exactly what Alex Ferguson has gone through and is still going through even now. It has been an absolute killer."

It took a joke own goal by Brian Gayle to leave Wilkinson's team laughing all the way to the championship.

Leeds' farcical match-winner seemed an appropriate way to settle the championship. Seldom, if ever, has the title been decided by a more ludicrous series of flukes and mishaps.

While Leeds may not be the classiest champions of all time, Wilkinson deserves the honour of becoming the first manager since Don Revie to bring back the glory days to Elland Road – and that is no mean feat.

Leeds have captured championship glory just three-and-a-half years after Wilkinson hauled the sleeping giant of Yorkshire from the jaws of relegation to the Third Division.

Yesterday's High Noon confrontation at Bramall Lane epitomised the thrills and spills of this year's title race.

Four of the five goals were either flukes, own goals or Leeds taking advantage of Sheffield's one-legged keeper!

And after leading his side to the top for the third time this season, he said: "I'm very, very proud, not just because we're in first place again but the way we did it.

"The image of this club means a lot to me and to turn in a performance like that in front of millions on TV was tremendous.

"It was our best display of the season and to be out there as captain was a great feeling."

Strachan's ingenuity opened the second half limping. The opening goal set the pattern for the fun that followed.

John Gannon's corner created havoc in the Leeds defence after 29 minutes and in the mad scramble, Alan Cork swivelled and shot past John Lukic.

As the first half moved into injury time Gordon Strachan's quickly-taken free-kick allowed Danny Wallace to chip the ball over Rees.

Skipper Gayle attempted to whack the ball clear, but it first struck Gary Speed, bounced across the open goal and then spun off Wallace into the net.

Gary McAllister's free kick sailed over the limping keeper to the far post where full-back Jon Newsome headed in after 64 minutes.

Leeds' lead survived just three minutes before United were level.

Gannon's corner again caused problems and when John Pemberton cut the ball back, Chapman sliced it into his own net.

With 12 minutes left, a Leeds attack should have been little trouble for Gayle.

However, Rees hobbled out to the edge of his area where Gayle leaped to head the ball over his keeper and into the empty net.

Mel Rees so badly damaged his right knee when Leeds equalised seconds before half-time that he spent the entire

SHEFF UTD 2
LEEDS UTD 3

MIRROR SPORT

SAY THE LEEDS and you're smiling

SKIPPER Gordon Strachan (left) leads the United celebrations after their third goal. Gary McAllister, Chris Fairclough, scorer Lee Chapman, Rodney Wallace and David Batty join the leaders' victory march

ASTON VILLA 1 LEEDS 4

Gordon roasts Big Ron

By JOHN EDWARDS

GORDON STRACHAN put his old boss Ron Atkinson through televised torture as Leeds stormed back to the First Division summit yesterday.

The little Scot gave Leeds' public image the perfect face-lift with an inspirational performance that enthralled millions of TV viewers.

But while it had manager Howard Wilkinson and a huge travelling support beaming broadly, it left his former Old Trafford boss shaking his head in disbelief.

Atkinson's Villa side went into the televised showdown on a roll of five straight League wins that had hoisted them from 11th to fourth. Yet they

THE TOP OF THE FIRST

	P	W	D	L	F	A	Pt
Leeds Utd	17	10	4	3	33	13	34
Man Utd	16	10	5	1	25	8	35
Man City	17	9	3	5	24	19	30
Aston Villa	17	8	5	4	23	19	27
C Palace	16	8	5	3	26	20	27
Arsenal	16	7	4	5	21	21	25

were given such a drubbing that the Villa manager was forced to concede: "We've had our backsides kicked.

"They gave us a good spanking, and on the evidence of that they are the best team we've seen all season.

"They showed belief and organisation, and when you see Strachan and Gary McAllister back-heeling the ball to each other you wonder whether our pitch is really that bad after all."

"I always call Strachan the greatest winger in the world.

and he still looks the part. His craft and enthusiasm are magnificent and I'm not the least bit surprised he's still maintaining his standards.

Strachan's impish skills inspired a victory that amounted to a public flogging.

And after leading his side to the top for the third time this season, he said: "I'm very, very proud, not just because we're in first place again but the way we did it.

"The image of this club means a lot to me and to turn in a performance like that in front of millions on TV was tremendous.

"It was our best display of the season and to be out there as captain was a great feeling."

Strachan's ingenuity opened

◄ Turn to Page 31

CHAMPIONS

DAILY Mirror PICTURE POWER

⚽ DELIGHTED Jon Newsome is hailed a hero after scoring Leeds' vital second goal at Bramall Lane yesterday.

⚽ It put Howard Wilkinson's side on the road to victory and the coveted League title.

Pics: ALBERT COOPER and PHIL SPENCER

DAILY MIRROR, Wednesday, January 8, 1992   Page 30

EMLYN HUGHES ON THE MOST

WHY I WANT

Sky high for Don

DON HOWE became Coventry City's new boss last night after winning a desperate game of double bluff with the club's directors.

HORROR

HOWARD WILKINSON (top) is reporting Leeds' title bid and Emlyn hopes Alex Ferguson takes the honours this season

● ELLAND ROAD

DAILY MIRROR, Wednesday, January 8, 1992   Page 31

TALKED ABOUT CLUB IN FOOTBALL

TO SEE LEEDS

'Revie's legacy taints them forever'

'Wilko's magic can't repair damage'

The hard men
DON REVIE and his skipper Billy Bremner led Leeds to success, but left a bad taste after

TORN APART!

WINNERS: Bremner lifts the FA Cup in 1972   **NEW BREED:** Howard Wilkinson and skipper Gordon Strachan

Schooled

Slick Hick

From BRUCE SMITH

IS STILL HOSTILE TERRITORY'

205

And Finally, A Message To The Budding Leeds Stars…

Trainer Les Cocker spells out the do's and don'ts to the Leeds United youngsters of 1963.

DON'T

FISH AND CHIPS
CHOCOLATES
CREAM CAKES

FRIED FOODS
GENERALLY
POP. (FIZZY)

NIGHTS

RLS

}IN EXCESS

LEEDS
MEDICAL

ACKNOWLEDGEMENTS:
This book is dedicated to my family – wife Pam and children Richard and Rebecca.
I must thank Richard Havers, editor of the *When Football Was Football* series, for inviting me to take on this project.

It wouldn't have happened without the blessing of my editor at the *Sunday Mirror*, Tina Weaver. And thanks also to my colleagues on the sports desk there who've indulged me in my reminiscences about Leeds.

Much of the research for the book was provided by Alex Walters and David Scripps of Mirrorpix. Their assistance was invaluable. Some of the *Mirror* staff photographers who took these pictures have passed away. I knew most of them. They were fine, talented men and are sorely missed. Their work stands up to scrutiny today.

Finally I must thank all the friends I made during my many years working with and reporting on Leeds United. Most of the people are publicly unknown, some famous and some of them infamous! They know who they are. They were all part of something very special.